Marilyn

THE QUEST
FOR AN OSCAR

JAMES TURIELLO

published by

a sandy beach

DERBY, CONNECTICUT

Marilyn Monroe: The Quest for an Oscar
Copyright © 2016 James Turiello. All Rights Reserved.

Published in the USA by
A Sandy Beach
22 East Court
Derby, CT 06418

ISBN-10: 0692603883
ISBN-13: 978-0692603888

Designed by duffincreative.com

Printed in the United States of America

Table of Contents

Billy Wilder:

"The luminosity of that face! There has never been a woman with such voltage on the screen, with the exception of Garbo."

Groucho Marx:

"It's amazing. She's Mae West, Theda Bara and Bo Peep all rolled into one".

Marilyn Monroe:

"This industry should behave like a mother whose child has just run out in front of a car. But instead of clasping the child to them, they start punishing the child. Like you don't dare get a cold. How dare you get a cold! I mean, the executives can get colds and stay home forever and phone it in, but how dare you, the actor, get a cold or a virus. You know, no one feels worse than the one who's sick. I sometimes wish, gee, I wish they had to act a comedy with a temperature and a virus infection."

Dedicated to Ebie, who showed me the world, took me to all the places
Marilyn longed to visit. The tropical paradises, with their emerald waters
and white sandy beaches.
To the little towns and the big cities, to adventures beyond description…..
and always filled my days and nights with undying love…

Foreword

"It takes a smart brunette to play a dumb blonde."

EVEN THOUGH MARILYN MONROE is credited with appearing in only thirty-three motion pictures, the legacy of Marilyn Monroe is so widespread it has and will endure for all time. Some of those thirty-three motion pictures had the unique distinction of becoming movie classics. The list of those feature films contains dramas, action adventures, film noir and even comedies. Marilyn was really a natural and from the very first time you caught a glimpse of that unforgettable look, smile, walk and sultry voice, it was apparent she was truly incomparable. The fact of the matter is that in the very first movies on the list of Marilyn Monroe feature films, she was not even listed in the credits. However, when you exited the theater you kept wondering who that girl was, who was she? Well you probably didn't even remember the scene she was in. You kept seeing that face, that smile, it glowed. You settled in at home or maybe decided to eat at some fancy restaurant and her image and voice kept rolling around in your mind. The next day at work you probably told all of your fellow workers about "the girl" in the movie. The girl in the movie was Marilyn Monroe and now you had to find out who she was and more importantly, where you could see more of her. Now it's over fifty years since her very untimely passing and Marilyn Monroe is without question the single most recognizable movie actress Hollywood has ever produced. That fact of fame is not relegated to only Hollywood and the United States but the entire world. Everyone knows her by only the mention of her first name, Marilyn. Some of the great movies that Marilyn Monroe starred in are classics, because Marilyn was in the cast. Enduring motion pictures such as *Some Like It Hot*, *The Misfits*, *Bus Stop*, *Niagara*, *The Seven Year Itch*, to name a few. It takes a very great and memorable performance to get nominated for an Academy Award and then if you are lucky, actually win one.

This book is not an autobiography, there are countless books about Marilyn Monroe that have already been published and cover that part of her short life. There will be no references to any gossip or speculation about how Hollywood's brightest star left Hollywood and the world before you could blink your eye. In the pages that follow Marilyn Monroe's performances will be evaluated and compared to the performances that the Academy and its members felt were more deserving of a nomination for the Oscar. For hard as it to believe, Marilyn Monroe was never even nominated for an Oscar. The many reasons that can be attributed to that startling fact will be covered in the pages that follow and hopefully you will be convinced that beyond a shadow of a doubt the incomparable Marilyn Monroe truly deserves an Oscar. The author has been on a campaign for the last several years to have the Academy of Motion Pictures Arts and Sciences award Oscars to some of the great Hollywood actors and actresses of the golden years who were so wrongly overlooked. The author even went so far as to offer a suggestion to open a museum dedicated to the placement of the Oscars that would be awarded to the stars who are no longer with us. In 2013 during the Oscar ceremony it appears someone was listening because an announcement was made that a museum dedicated to the fine art of film making is scheduled to open in 2016. Hopefully one of the highlights when they have their grand opening will be the addition of an honorary Oscar bearing the name Marilyn Monroe. Of course let's not forget that her male counterpart, the great swashbuckler Errol Flynn also deserves an honorary Oscar, and he too should be recognized on opening night at the museum ceremony.

When you come across a movie that Marilyn Monroe was in, it is encouraged that while you are watching her character, you evaluate the performance as if you were a movie critic. Then you can make your own conclusions to determine if Marilyn should have been recognized in that particular role. It is important that you approach the exercise with an open mind. Marilyn Monroe became a woman, an actress that everyone in Hollywood, her fellow actors and actresses, as well as, producers and directors could never stop thinking about. Then Marilyn Monroe became an iconic figure that everyone in the world knew and wanted to see more of her work. From her humble beginnings as a mere walk on contract player for two studios, 20th Century Fox and Columbia Pictures, to her final work for the very same 20th Century Fox Studio. It might have been her biggest movie of all time, *Something's Got To Give*, with Dean Martin, Cyd Charisse, and Tom Tryon. The movie remains an unfinished film that showed Marilyn Monroe as a star that still was generating sparks as she graced the screen. Marilyn Monroe never looked better, more beautiful and voluptuous than ever before. That year was 1962, and now over fifty years later Marilyn Monroe is ever present. She can be found in collectables of every shape and form, as well as, hundreds of magazine covers and countless documentaries that are still being made. Even restaurants are opening over the globe bearing her name, featuring their entire décor dedicated to Marilyn. Get ready to take a journey with Marilyn Monroe as she became the most recognizable movie star that Hollywood ever created. This is a journey you will never forget.

CHAPTER 1

The Two Marilyns

"No one ever told me I was pretty when I was a little girl.
All little girls should be told they're pretty, even if they aren't."

WHEN A PERSON THINKS OF THE 1920's and 1930's and even the 1940's most people refer to them as the good old days. It is true the most of those years were filled with hardship, but in the good old USA it was during one of those most famous decades that a very special baby girl by the name of Norma Jeane Mortenson was born. The year was 1926. The place where that special baby girl was born was not in some big city like New York, Dallas Texas or Miami Florida, the place was a very small section in the charity ward at the Los Angeles County Hospital. That tiny little baby girl would go on to become the most celebrated Hollywood star, as well as, the most recognizable actresses of all time. That tiny little baby girl would become a movie icon with no equal. That tiny little baby girl would become Marilyn Monroe. It is important to reflect on Marilyn Monroe's, or Norma Jeane's, very humble and unlikely beginning when evaluating Marilyn Monroe's acting ability. How does an individual who had such a troubled beginning with her childhood, which can only be described as volatile, become so very famous. A childhood that included Marilyn Monroe being passed from family members to family friends and frequently staying in orphanages as a result of her mother's mental health. Finally, all of the family members and family friends decided that in order to avoid another orphanage stay for Marilyn, they thought it would be best to have the then only sixteen year old Marilyn Monroe married off. They had a guy all lined up and as it turned out he was quickly sent to the Pacific as a merchant marine shortly after their hurried marriage. Marilyn Monroe, or Norma Jeane then began working on an assembly line at an aeronautical plant. It is highly likely you already know this part of Marilyn Monroe's story and also the fact that in 1945 a photographer took a snapshot of the stunning brunette while she was still working at that plant. It is a most important part of the historical details of Marilyn Monroe's early beginnings because they actually play an important role in her development as a great movie star. Yes, that famous photo shoot led to Marilyn Monroe becoming a successful model, securing dozens of magazine covers and even a screen test with 20th Century Fox. The studio executives, directors and those photographers knew from their first encounter that she had a unique ability to capture and hold the attention of anyone on the opposite end of a camera lens. That little baby girl began her life as Norma Jeane Mortenson, as a dark haired brunette, but before she was twenty one years old she became a platinum haired blond with the name Marilyn Monroe.

In the years that followed everything about that little baby girl was unique, and she became even more iconic than any other woman in the world at that time by having the distinction of being recognized by just one name, Marilyn. The fame that followed Marilyn Monroe throughout her very short time in Hollywood was so great that everyone in the whole world knew exactly who you were talking about when you said her name. Hollywood has always been fond of compiling lists of the best of this or that. Then why

LIFE

THERE IS A CASE
FOR INTERPLANETARY
SAUCERS

MARILYN MONROE
THE TALK OF HOLLYWOOD

20 CENTS

APRIL 7, 1952

is it that Marilyn Monroe, who is very high on one of the most prestigious lists, The 50 Greatest Screen Legends, was never nominated for an Oscar. The American Film Institute, who released the list the "50 Greatest Screen Legends," ranked Marilyn Monroe as number six amongst the actresses, ahead of the great Elizabeth Taylor, who was number seven. For the record, it was one of Hollywood's greatest female stars, Katherine Hepburn, who made it to number one. In one respect Marilyn Monroe was good enough to be considered as having enough talent to rank among other legendary Hollywood actresses, but not enough talent to be considered for awards. Even Playboy, the most recognized glamour magazine in the world named Marilyn Monroe an unprecedented number one on their list of "The 100 Sexiest Stars of the Century". Another big magazine, Entertainment Weekly, compiled a list of the top 100 entertainers of all time, and Marilyn came in third. It was a very big honor for Marilyn, because The Beatles were ranked number one and Elvis was ranked number two.

One of the most famous traditions in all of Hollywood is for famous actors and actresses to have their handprints or footprints immortalized into the cement in front of Grauman's Chinese Theater. When it was Marilyn Monroe's day to be honored with Jane Russell, it was a very special day. The main reason that made it so special was, of course, the public appearance of Marilyn Monroe and to this day it stands as the most popular Chinese Theater ceremonies of all time. It had the largest turnout of not only fans, but members of the media and press as well. One of the most famous of all the popular picture magazines in the United States was Life magazine. If you made the cover of Life, it was said you were a big star or a very prominent personality. Well Marilyn Monroe added to her list of unique major accomplishments with a record number of cover appearances on Life Magazine. Marilyn made the cover of Life magazine, April 7, 1952, May 25, 1953, April 20, 1959, November 9, 1959, August 15, 1960, June 22, 1962, August 17, 1962, August 8, 1964, and December 22, 1969. That was the most Life covers for any of the actresses during her era as a star. It should be noted though, that the issues after her untimely death in 1962 were memorial issues. The other big magazine during that era was Time magazine and Marilyn also graced the cover for the May 14, 1956 issue. When an actor or actress is constantly being featured in magazine articles, and can boast about a very high number on important lists of achievements, such as the ones that have been described, it confirms that they have been embraced by the public. It really doesn't describe how good or bad they were as an actor or actress, it could only mean that they were extremely popular. The case of her extreme popularity has been made regarding Marilyn Monroe, but to really delve into the prospect of whether Marilyn Monroe was deserving of an Oscar nomination, or perhaps even a win, needs much more evaluation. One of Hollywood's all time experts in performing that type of evaluation did just that in regard to Marilyn Monroe. Most people involved in the movie industry regard him as the father of method acting in America. He was not only an actor himself, but a director, as well as, an acting teacher. The person who I am describing is none other than Lee Strasberg. Lee Strasberg revolutionized the art of acting by having a profound influence on performance in both the American theater, as well as, the entire movie industry. Mr. Strasberg's school in New York had many, many famous students. When you think of the giants of Hollywood actors and actresses the following are just some who came out of his training, Iconic names like James Dean, Paul Newman, Anne Bancroft, Montgomery Clift, Dustin Hoffman, Julie Harris, Al Pacino, even Robert DeNiro and director Elia Kazan. Yes, Elia Kazan was actually a student of Lee Strasberg, and both Elia Kazan and James Dean were nominated for Oscars for their respective work in *East of Eden*, the very first movie James Dean was in. The list of famous Hollywood individuals that were students at some time during their career, pupils of Lee Strasberg is much too long. In order to give more credibility of Strasberg's reputation to recognize and develop talent, another name comes to mind, Sidney Lumet, who was an American director, producer and screenwriter with over 50 films to his credit. As a student of Strasberg he was nominated for the Oscar as Best Director a total of four times. The movies were, *12 Angry Men, Dog Day Afternoon, Network and The Verdict*. In addition, 14 of his films were nominated for multiple Oscars, such as *Network*, which was nominated

for 10 awards, winning 4. Lee Strasberg even made a big mark as an actor and everyone remembers him for his role as the gangster Hyman Roth in *The Godfather Part II*. That iconic role earned him an Oscar nomination for Best Supporting Actor. It is very important to establish the biography of Lee Strasberg and his influence on the motion picture industry, because one of his favorite students was, none other than Marilyn Monroe. Lee Strasberg always had a fondness for Marilyn Monroe. He deeply admired her talent. Mr. Strasberg rated Marilyn Monroe as a close second to another one of his greatest students, Marlon Brando. Imagine that, Marilyn Monroe being compared to Hollywood's greatest actors by one of Hollywood's greatest influences. It was Lee Strasberg who gave a very poignant eulogy at Marilyn Monroe's funeral. "For us, Marilyn was a devoted and loyal friend, a colleague constantly reaching for perfection. We shared her pain and difficulties, and

some of her joys. She was a member of our family. It is difficult to accept the fact that her zest for life has been ended by this dreadful accident. Despite the heights and brilliance she had attained on the screen, she was planning for the future. She was looking forward to participating in the many exciting things. In her eyes, and in mine, her career was just beginning. She had a luminous quality. A combination of wistfulness, radiance, and yearning that set her apart and made everyone wish to be part of it, to share in the childish innocence which was at once so shy and yet so vibrant. This quality was even more evident when she was on the stage. I am truly sorry that the public who loved her did not have the opportunity to see her as we did, in many of

Dangerous Years, with William Halop (1947)

Ladies of the Chorus (1948)

the roles that foreshadowed what she would have become. Without a doubt she would have been one of the really great actresses on the stage." The most influential man in Hollywood during the time of Marilyn Monroe's career and development, Lee Strasberg, clearly recognized the talent that Marilyn possessed as an actress. Mr. Strasberg was not alone in his evaluation of Marilyn's performances on the big screen as some of her critics always had great things to say about the final product that Marilyn Monroe delivered. In many ways one could definitely say there really were two Marilyn's. One was just an everyday girl trying to live her life and be happy, that Marilyn had trouble finding happiness. The other Marilyn was a very unique movie star, a movie star that was unlike anyone the world had ever seen before. Maybe the combination of the two Marilyn's is what made Marilyn so special, so unforgettable and so iconic.

Marilyn had the distinction that even if only having a walk on part which she might have shared with Hollywood heavyweights, she is the one you remember. Before Marilyn Monroe made her first appearance on the big screen, and today over sixty-five years later there is no actress that can make that claim, the claim of having "it". The "it", the je ne sais quoi, the indefinable

Ladies of the Chorus (1948)

something that made Marilyn special. Another Hollywood heavyweight was fortunate to work with and direct the two Marilyn's, his name was Billy Wilder. He was an all-around personality in the same league as Lee Strasberg when it came to knowing talent. Billy Wilder was not only a producer and director, but also a writer. He has the distinction of being one of only five individuals who have won Oscars for writing, producing and directing, for the same film, *The Apartment*. To confirm just how great a movie personality Billy Wilder was, you only have to look at the list of other Oscars he won during his illustrious career. Billy won the Oscar for *The Lost Weekend, Sunset Boulevard, Stalag 17, Sabrina, Some Like It Hot,* (perhaps Marilyn's best performance), *The Apartment, Irma La Douce* and *The Fortune Cookie.* Even though Billy Wilder incurred numerous problems while trying to direct Marilyn Monroe in two blockbuster comedies, some of the comments he made after she died indicate once more how great her acting really was. Marilyn Monroe was notorious for being late on movie sets and even more notorious for leaving early. Billy Wilder knew these facts before working with her on two of his most memorable movies. The movies were both comedies and of course both big box office hits. The movies in question were, *The Seven Year Itch*, (1955), and *Some Like It Hot*, (1959). Keep in mind movie tickets during the 1950's were very inexpensive, but estimated box office receipts for *The Seven Year Itch*, was over 201 million dollars, and *Some Like It Hot*, brought in an amazing 232 million dollars. Those are very big numbers for any movie even for movies made today. Though Billy Wilder's comments have some criticism attached to them, they do reflect admiration for Marilyn Monroe as an actress. Billy Wilder said; "Whatever she threw away, we printed it, and it was very good. It was very, very good. She had a kind of elegant vulgarity about her. That, I think, was very important. And she automatically knew where the joke was. She did not discuss it. She came for the first rehearsal, and she was absolutely perfect. She had a feeling for and a fear of the camera. Fright. She also loved the camera. Whatever she did, wherever she stood, there was always that thing that comes through. She was not even aware of it." This quote gives you an idea of the aforementioned "it" factor that only Marilyn had.

Love Happy with Groucho Marx (1949)

Another iconic film director and producer during the golden age of movies who worked with the two Marilyn's was Howard Hawks. When you think of great science fiction movies, one stands out, *The Thing From Another World*. It was made in 1951 and produced and directed by Howard Hawks. He had quite a career before that movie was made and he took on the task of producing a musical which would have Marilyn Monroe as its star. He also has in his resume some classic westerns, such as *Red River, Rio Bravo*, and *El Dorado*, to attest to the overall versatility of Howard Hawks. The year was 1953 and the musical was, *Gentlemen Prefer Blondes*. His new star Marilyn Monroe proved to Mr. Hawks that the movie was going to be a big hit. In terms of box office it was not as big as some of Marilyn Monroe's other movies, but in 1953, the sum of 148 million dollars was an outstanding return for *Gentlemen Prefer Blondes*. Howard Hawks once described Marilyn Monroe as one of the most gifted and talented actresses he had ever worked with, mainly because she did everything so naturally. The movie *Gentleman Prefer Blondes* convinced Howard Hawks that, not only was Marilyn Monroe a great dramatic actress, but Marilyn was also a great comedic actress. Her delivery of lines like "Don't you know that a man being rich is like a girl being pretty? You wouldn't marry a girl just because she's pretty, but my goodness, doesn't it help?" and "I can be smart when it's important" show that perfectly. It was evident to Mr. Hawks that he was on the long list of great directors that Marilyn had already worked with and how she impressed them. Howard Hawks did not consider musicals as his forte, but his direction in *Gentleman Prefer Blondes* is undoubtedly some of his best work. It seemed that Marilyn Monroe somehow brought out some magical quality that always satisfied whoever she worked with. True, while the movie was being made she was not a joy to work with at times, but in the end the final product was what really mattered. Marilyn Monroe was so gifted that she made some of the musical numbers into timeless classics due to her sultry voice and fantastic delivery. There are many songs in this classic musical, but one in particular that Marilyn sings became her signature song. *Gentlemen Prefer Blondes* features Marilyn's memorable rendition of the now immortal "Diamonds Are a Girl's Best Friend," written by Jule Styn and Leo Robin. It has become one of those parts of a movie that once you see it you will never forget it. *Gentlemen Prefer Blondes* cemented Marilyn Monroe as 20th Century Fox's number one actress. Most critics felt strongly that Marilyn Monroe's performance brought something that they were missing since the days of Jean Harlow. It was much more of what Harlow had, including Marilyn's own style of delivering musical numbers. Finally they all agreed, Marilyn Monroe had the looks, but now they stated that she could act too, or put in another way there were really two Marilyn's.

Some of the other producers and directors who worked with Marilyn Monroe during her short illustrious career were, John Huston, Fritz Lang, Otto Preminger, Joshua Logan, Henry Hathaway, Joseph L. Mankiewicz and Lawrence Olivier, to name a few. Of special note is the way John Huston described working with Marilyn Monroe on his epic The Misfits. He was very upset at times by her constantly falling ill on set. However, Mr Huston also stated on numerous occasions, in spite of all the negative publicity about Marilyn during the making of the movie, he would be willing to work with her again. "When people talk about her", he said, "they are generally talking about themselves." "They don't really know her." He went on to say that Marilyn was one of the best actresses who he ever worked with and she deserved to be recognized for her ability to capture a moment, a scene, as it was magical. The aforementioned description of how Marilyn was able to impress the biggest producers, directors and fellow actors is a confirmation that she was deserving much more recognition than she received. There are of course many degrees to measure success. In Hollywood there is one and only one that insures success and recognition, The Oscar. The argument can be made that when one formidable director or producer strongly feels he has worked on a production where his star deserves a nomination, it usually becomes reality. The unfortunate facts remain that even though almost every one of the producers and directors that worked with Marilyn, shared various degrees of praise for her talents, none chose to push the envelope on her behalf. Marilyn always far exceeded their expectations but in the end she was always overlooked.

The Asphalt Jungle (1950)

CHAPTER 2

From Small Roles
to Leading Lady

*"Some people have been unkind. If I say I want to grow as an actress,
they look at my figure. If I say I want to develop, to learn my craft, they laugh.
Somehow they don't expect me to be serious about my work."*

MARILYN MONROE; when you hear that famous, iconic name many
glamorous and sexy images immediately enter your mind. In all the years
since Hollywood created the term leading lady, there is only one that has
lasted long after her untimely demise, a demise that was way back in 1962.
Just try to list each and every female leading lady that reached the status
of a major motion picture actress and it is certain that the list will be quite
long and will contain many unique and glamorous stars. However, if you also
decide to make a comparison between your list of female stars, it is a given
that even if you take the best quality of let's say five of the women on your

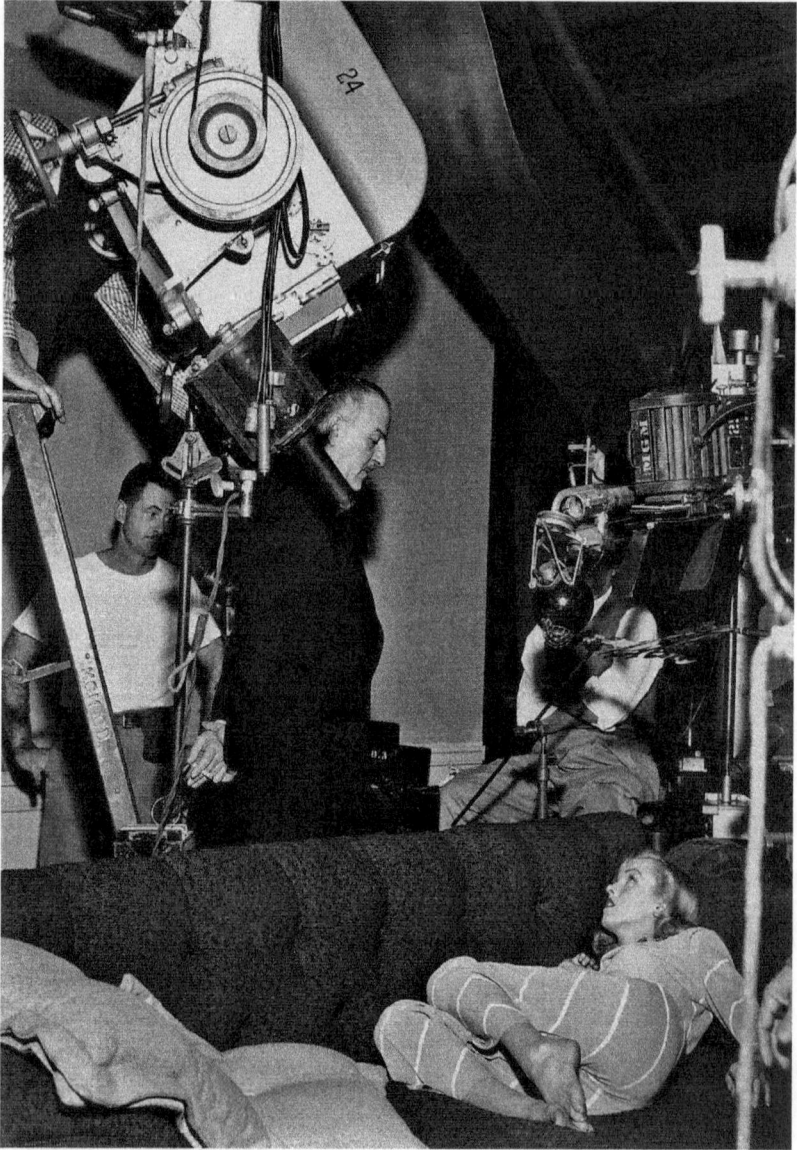

list, they will come up short in comparison to Marilyn Monroe. They will not be able to compare to Marilyn Monroe in sheer star quality or for Marilyn's dynamic personality traits. The word traits is used in the plural sense, because Marilyn Monroe did have many special traits. On the surface she was blessed with a beautiful face, complete with a special smile and a unique pout. Marilyn Monroe had a voluptuous body, a body that melted the hearts and souls of almost any man who laid eyes on it. If you happened to see a women walking away from you without ever seeing her face, and it happened to be Marilyn Monroe, you would know it was her. It goes without saying that she had a unique and special sexy walk that will never be duplicated. How about when Marilyn Monroe spoke, how about the sultry way she pronounced her words. It was just her way of being Marilyn. When she said goodbye, she gave you "that wink". As you can see Marilyn Monroe was the total package, and it was a package that reached across all of the seven continents. That special persona and name that is still universal around the world and never lost its iconic popularity. Travel abroad, and for sure when you enter a gift shop or clothing boutique there will be some image or collectable or even a clothing line that features Marilyn Monroe's image. From a literary standpoint there has never been a movie actress that has had even a quarter of the number of books written about them, then the number of books written about Marilyn Monroe. Then why attempt to write another book about a woman that has been written about so often? The main reason is to evaluate and try to allow the reader to examine the performances that Marilyn Monroe gave to her fans. The mere fact that somehow the Academy of Movie Arts and Sciences failed to nominate Marilyn Monroe for even one Oscar, is a travesty. It's not beyond the realm of possibility that they will feel the way you will after taking a closer look at Marilyn Monroe as an actress and then grant her an Oscar for her complete body of work. It is a body of work that is filled with outstanding dramatic performances. A body of work with pure perfection in her comedic performances. A body of work that includes musical renditions delivered by Marilyn Monroe that rival some of the most gifted female vocalists. Marilyn Monroe songs from her movies are almost like tiny little time machines that for certain will take you back to when you first heard them. It all came together in a unique magical way, the pout, the look, the hair, the body, the walk, and finally, the sadness in her eyes. When Marilyn Monroe was just starting to get noticed for even her minor movie roles in the movies, it was not unusual to see her image on the cover of multiple magazines every single month. When you went to a newsstand to buy the daily paper, there were always a dozen magazines with Marilyn on the cover looking at you. Today, and all the years since her untimely death, there are literally hundreds and hundreds of magazines that still feature her iconic image. It was of course the photo of Marilyn Monroe on the very first issue of Playboy that gave the magazine the jumpstart that has propelled it for decades as the number one men's magazine of all time. Keep in mind that the most sought after calendar photo that made Marilyn Monroe a household name back in the late 1940's, actually was the first appearance of Marilyn Monroe on a calendar and today that legacy is still alive. Each and every year there are many companies that still produce Marilyn Monroe calendars and they are right at the top of the best seller list of all calendars.

When it comes to being the number one most recognizable movie actress and unquestionable the most glamorous movie actress of all time, Marilyn Monroe is the first and only name that comes to mind and we have not even touched on her outstanding performances. The roles that Marilyn took on with only one thing in mind, creating memorable, distinctive characters. If you evaluate the movies from 1948, the year was filled with westerns, these cowboy movies were much more than the usual 'shoot em' up fare. They were action packed dramas, some of which are considered classic movies today. Great western sagas, dramatic masterpieces. *Red River, 3 Godfathers, Fort Apache*, and *The Treasure of the Sierra Madre*, always filled the seats in all of the movie theaters where they were shown. The movie patrons knew when they left the theater, they got their money's worth. Also on the list of memorable box office giants were even more action movies such as *The Pirate, The Black Arrow, The Three Musketeers* and *The Adventures of Don Juan*. There were also some notable comedies, such as, *Abbott and Costello Meet Frankenstein*, and

With Louis Calhern in T*he Asphalt Jungle* (1950)

Bob Hope in *The Paleface.* These movies always entertained and they all turned a huge profit for their respective studios. One of the movies mentioned was so outstanding, *The Treasure of the Sierra Madre*, it even won the Oscar for Best Picture. Best Director Oscar went to John Huston and Best Supporting Actor Oscar was won by Walter Huston. The movie-going public was enamored with action, adventure, comedy and drama, but musicals were not very popular, and certainly not box office money makers. Marilyn Monroe happened to be a part of that unique year because it turned out that the musical, *Ladies of the Chorus*, was Marilyn Monroe's very first starring role, but most of her fans have never had the pleasure of seeing just how good this young and new actress really was. The musical is now thought of as being a hidden gem, and most critics of today agree with the ones who reviewed it way back in 1948, that it's a very well-made tight little musical. It is only one hour in length and Marilyn Monroe was virtually a complete unknown at the

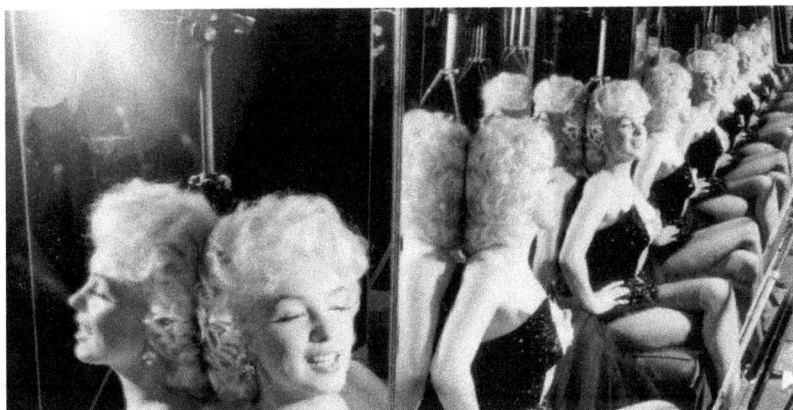

time, with only a sparse resume of extra work to her credit. Marilyn only had one other real credited small part when she was cast in this movie. When you watch it for the first time you will be amazed that she's the same Marilyn Monroe that graced the screen years later that everyone is so familiar with. When it is said that she is the same Marilyn Monroe, you the viewer, will see for yourself that Marilyn was not only being Marilyn, but her iconic presence was evident. It was very difficult for any young and unseasoned actress to attack a role that had both dramatic scenes, as well as, song and dance numbers. Marilyn Monroe stars as a very young burlesque chorus girl who works in the chorus alongside her mother played by Adele Jergens. When one of the stars of the show walks out, Marilyn gets her part and becomes an overnight sensation, earning the interest of many men. One very wealthy heir played by the handsome Rand Brooks, falls deeply in love with Marilyn. The movie has some intrigue added when the mother, Adele Jergens, fears that Marilyn's character will never be accepted by his social circles. The fear stems from her own past experience with her troubled annulled marriage to a socially prominent young man decades ago. As you can imagine a lot happens in a mere sixty minutes, but Marilyn handles all the drama, and even sings two surprisingly good songs for a "B" movie, "Anyone Can See I Love You" and "Every Baby Needs a Da Da Daddy". It can also be said that the latter is a sexy little number that will remind everyone of Marilyn's classic rendition of

"Diamonds are a Girl's Best Friend" with her unique delivery that mesmerized men of all ages. Columbia Pictures used Adele Jergens in many of their movies and she was given top billing in the original 1948 release, but when the movie was re-released in 1952, Columbia decided to take full advantage of Marilyn's rising star power and gave her top billing. The leading man, Rand Brooks, played Scarlett O'Hara's first husband in *Gone With The Wind* and he was completely taken in by the evident sexiness and beauty of Marilyn Monroe, but even more so by her ability to be more versatile than most actresses he had previously worked with. This is by far a movie that will be hard to find because of the year it was made, as well as, the fact that most T.V. movie networks shied away from such short productions. However, it is one that must get a much closer look when making a claim that Marilyn Monroe's body of work is deserving of Oscar consideration. This movie has been evaluated mainly because if you watch the movie a few times, you will clearly see how Marilyn Monroe had raw talent. She was able to completely mesmerize the audience and really give a memorable and good performance. Two years before that memorable dramatic and entertaining debut, Hollywood decided to test the water so to speak, and produce a very controversial and sexy feature film. The cast was unique and featured John Garfield who was one of Hollywood's bad

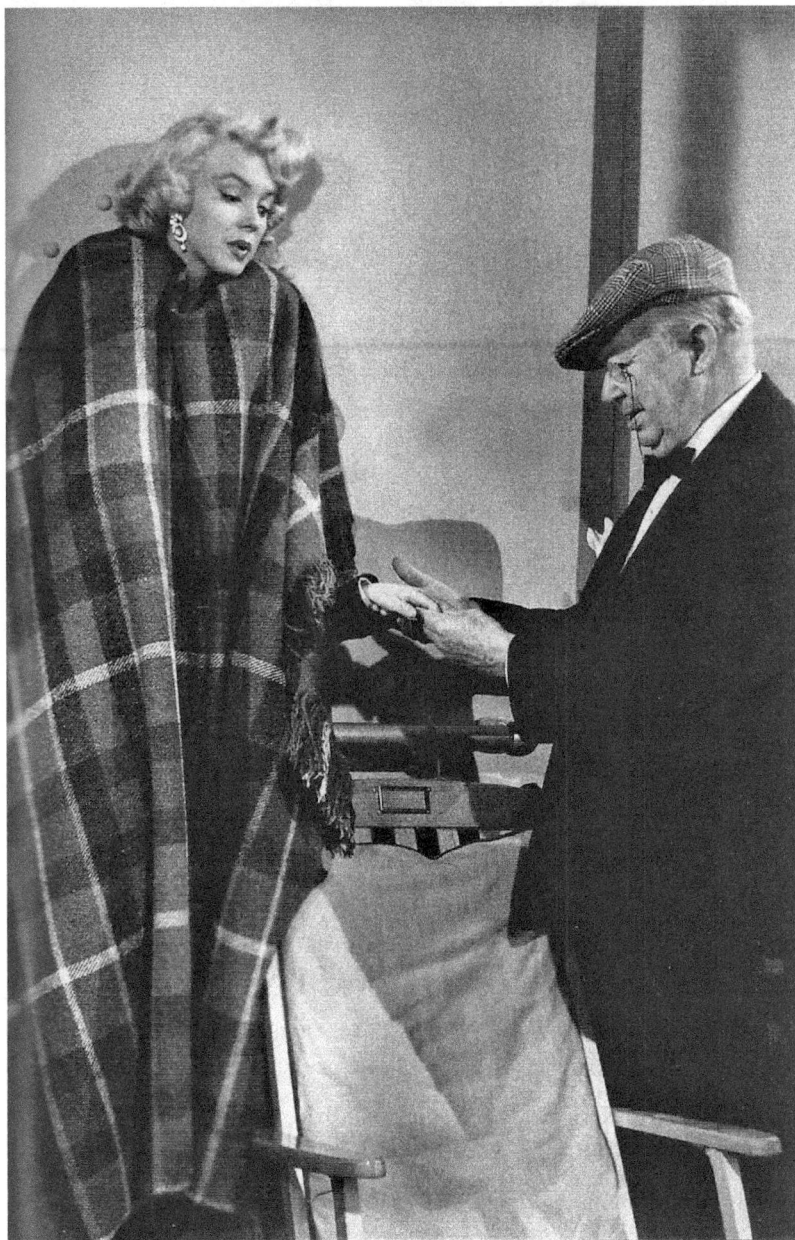

The Fireball with Mickey Rooney (1950)

boy actors and their most revered female sex symbol, Lana Turner. The movie
was *The Postman Always Rings Twice*. It is a shame that during the making
of this melodrama Marilyn Monroe was still an unknown, who really didn't
have her sights set on Hollywood, but was thrust on the scene and hired
by 20th Century Fox Studios in early 1946. It was a series of now famous
photo shoots that led Marilyn to the studio. Getting back to the great film
noir production, *The Postman Always Rings Twice*, Lana Turner as the star,
was absolutely the perfect actress to cast as the seductive Cora. There was no
doubt right from the first scene that featured Lana Turner and John Garfield
that the sparks really did fly. Throughout the production it was apparent
that they both truly enjoyed their respective roles, however, when it came
time for Oscar nominations, neither one got the slightest buzz. It seems that
Hollywood, when recognizing its stars' performances, there is certainly quite
a bit that goes into the mix. Both of these stars would later be nominated for

best actress and best actor awards, but neither star was able to take home the Oscar. It would be an interesting scenario if instead of Lana Turner it was Marilyn Monroe in the title role. The picture would have been the perfect beginning to Marilyn's career, and if she was around and one of the female actresses who were being considered for the role, it is an almost a guarantee that the part would have been given to Marilyn. It is a very long shot but try to visualize her beautiful face, hair and her voluptuous body being seen for the very first time as John Garfield enters the restaurant and meets Cora. It would have been monumental. The role was tailor made for Marilyn. There is no doubt she would have sent sparks from the screen and more important, maybe even nominated for her first Oscar.

Right Cross (1950)

Even though Marilyn Monroe began her movie career as a femme fatale and was originally thought of as pure eye candy, it was apparent that early in her career she had a flare for the dramatic, and was a scene stealer. The very first appearances that Marilyn Monroe had on the big screen, were very small roles that Marilyn somehow made memorable. They always left the viewer in awe and most thought to themselves, "Who was that girl." The movie going

public told their friends about Marilyn and how you must see that girl. Consider how uneventful these very first roles were, most were just mere walk on parts with absolutely no dialog. However, even without a script to memorize Marilyn Monroe was meticulous in her way of approaching the opportunity to be on the big screen. Marilyn in her own unique way made sure she was not only going to be noticed, but that she also had it in her mind that you the viewer would never, ever forget that girl. The unique factor about Marilyn's approach to these early appearances is that the combination of her natural abilities, coupled with her dedication to make an impression was dynamic. She wanted to be an actress, but had no idea that without even trying she already was one, a very special one. One of Hollywood's biggest and most profound ladies man was the inimitable Groucho Marx. He had a reputation for his way with the ladies. In one of his many comedies, Groucho is asked the question that everyone remembers today, "Why are you always chasing women?". Groucho answered, "I'll tell you as soon as I catch one". Here in a twist of fate, the paths of Marilyn and Groucho crossed, unexpectedly. The following is an account of the very first meeting between this seasoned ladies man, a connoisseur of women, and an innocent movie extra. How did the great Groucho react? This is still another example of how special Marilyn Monroe was, even if it was only walking into a room. The year was 1949, Groucho was making a movie called, *Love Happy*. One day the producer called Groucho and told him that he had to pick a girl from some extras, for a short scene the next day. Marilyn was one of the extra girls that Groucho would have to select from. The following is an account of what transpired in Groucho's own words. Keep in mind that in 1949 Groucho Marx was one of Hollywood's biggest comedic stars and had his movies were always in the top grossing films during his era. Groucho was ready for the mini audition and the first young lady walked across the room, Groucho checked her over and waited for the second young lady. He looked her over carefully and eagerly awaited for number three. After the third young lady walked by Groucho, the director looked at Groucho and said, "Well which one?". "Are you kidding me", Groucho said, "number three, when she walked the whole room revolved". That third young lady was Marilyn Monroe. Groucho, in an interview in the mid-sixties stated Marilyn Monroe was paid only one hundred dollars for that short scene and he went on to say, "she was a very sweet young girl and he had the highest regard for her". *Love Happy*, is the seventh movie that has Marilyn Monroe listed in the credits, but most likely the one that really got her noticed by the Hollywood big boys. For example, a poster from this Marx Brothers movie stated, "This is the picture that discovered Marilyn Monroe", and has two seductive images of Marilyn next to the faces of the Marx Brothers. Even though that mini audition landed her a short walk on role, her promotional value eclipsed the famous Marx Brothers. That in itself was a major accomplishment for Marilyn, who was still a relative unknown. In some of the other middle to late 1940's movies that Marilyn was featured in, she also had only seconds on the screen. Short scenes, such as a girl in a canoe, in *Scudda Hoo! Scudda Hay!* Even a very quick scene in *Green Grass of Wyoming*, as a square dancer, people who saw her in that movie, all were wondering who in the world was that girl. All in all, if you need some other indication of why Marilyn should be recognized for her later performances, one of these early ones is a great place to begin. Just before her chance meeting with the great Groucho Marx in *Love Happy*, that other movie musical, *Ladies of the Chorus*, had Marilyn cast in a major role, but it too got some more positive exposure for Marilyn. The movie was only a short one hour B-movie, but the critics were all in agreement that this very young and beautiful actress that goes by the name of Marilyn, has something very special.

As the new decade of the 1950's began, Marilyn was beginning to raise eyebrows and was getting noticed by the public. When the public embraces a brand new talent such as they embraced Marilyn, Hollywood reacts. Even though it was apparent that she was able to captivate the movie going public with only mediocre roles she was cast in, the studio failed to use her talent properly and give her more meaty roles that would utilize her acting skills. It seemed that Marilyn would be relegated to a regime of lackluster B-movies that would keep her in this mold throughout the decade of the 1950's. For

example, in 1951 Hollywood was in the midst of a slew of some of the best movies they have ever produced to date. It was a year that brought such classics as, *A Streetcar Named Desire*, *The African Queen*, and *A Place in the Sun*. It was also a year and time when horror and science fiction movies were much more than just B-movie quickies and some have become classics that are still popular today. Movie goers flocked to the theater to see, *The Day The Earth Stood Still*, and *The Thing from Another World*. In the first year of her renewed contract with 20th Century Fox, Marilyn Monroe made four movies. All four were movies with little or no substance and even though Marilyn approached them with her usual eagerness, the scripts were not memorable. The movies that Marilyn was in had titles like, *Home Town Story*, *Love Nest*, *As Young as you Feel* and *Let's Make it Legal*. All four movies are only worth discussing because of the fact that Marilyn Monroe was in the cast. One movie, *Home Town Story*, was actually suppose to be of all things, an automobile commercial. The total time that Marilyn is in the movie is less than two minutes. Another one of those 1951 movies Marilyn was in, *Let's Make it Legal*, was a comedy but not one that generated much laughter. If you blink your eyes you might just miss Marilyn. Sad to say, this feature was just one more movie that the studio placed Marilyn in a miscast role that could really be considered as merely a cameo appearance by today's standards. The fourth and final movie Marilyn was in during that period of her career was, *As Young as you Feel*. The tabloids wrote, "Newcomer Marilyn Monroe, shines, (glows is a better word) in a charming small role". The movie did do quite well at the box office, mainly because it had such a massive publicity build-up from Fox. The studio focused in attracting Marilyn's fans. It worked, because of one factor, Marilyn was in it. She had a small, but choice role, as a curvy secretary who knows her effects on men. If you look at the current artwork on the DVD release of all four of the 1951 movies Marilyn was in, only Marilyn Monroe is on the cover artwork. Marilyn was only on screen for a very short time in each one, but it appears these are movies with Marilyn as the star. In addition to these credits, Marilyn was rumored to have appeared as an extra in some additional movies, but no exact list exists. Some film buffs claim she appears in the musical comedies, *The Shocking Miss Pilgrim* (her voice as a telephone operator), *You Were Meant for Me* and even in a western, *Green Grass of Wyoming* (an extra at a square dance), but these claims are unconfirmed, yet they are mentioned on IMDB.

Marilyn Monroe's studio decided to take advantage of what the critics had wrote about their new actress and she received several roles in the decade of the 1950's. There were no less than five more movie credits to Marilyn's name during that period of her career. *A Ticket to Tomahawk,* and *Right Cross* are both listed as uncredited small roles. The other three movies that have Marilyn Monroe in the credits truly made Hollywood and the general public take notice that Marilyn was a unique and genuine star, and their initial impressions proved to be more than correct. The first of these movies was a highly acclaimed crime drama, *The Asphalt Jungle*, a neat piece of film noir directed by one of Hollywood's finest directors, John Huston. Mr. Huston remembered Marilyn over a decade later and he cast her in another one of his iconic movies, *The Misfits. Asphalt Jungle* was a crime drama which had a great cast and featured big and not so big names of the 1950's. There was Sterling Hayden in the lead role with, Jean Hagen, James Whitmore, Sam Jaffe, Louis Calhern, Anthony Caruso, Brad Dexter, John Maxwell, and John McIntire to name just a few. It was Marilyn who had a very minor, but a very key role in the plot who truly made her presence known again. John Huston was a director who felt the importance of selecting the casts for his movies to insure the movie would be memorable. To Mr. Huston, each movie he directed was a work of art. This trait insured that the individuals he selected could bring to the screen all the intricate aspects of the role they portrayed. In *The Asphalt Jungle* he demonstrated that fact, because each of the characters definitely had their specific moment in the movie. It was apparent that even the small character roles stood out, in a John Huston production. Even if for only one or even several scenes, they all had a presence. In the case of Marilyn she was up for the task and regardless of how minute her lines or time on the screen was, Marilyn performed like a seasoned actress. Once again had Marilyn Monroe been given the opportunity to be the star in any movie at

this time in her career, it is certain she would have been more than able to get a nomination, if the role was a memorable one. It might sound a little far-fetched and prejudiced, but it will be up to you to decide when you choose to revisit Marilyn's movies. When this movie was being promoted, as was the case in Hollywood at the time, movie posters were a major part of the promotion, there were no television movie trailers like the ones that are common-place today. The poster for *The Asphalt Jungle* had a picture of Marilyn with some names of the stars of the cast, but her name was not included. Upon a closer look at the poster Marilyn's image is the largest and this was the beginning for her iconic images to reach all of the media. The artwork for *The Asphalt Jungle* features an image of the reclining Marilyn Monroe, a testimony perhaps of one of the most important scenes in the movie. John Huston many

years later remarked that he felt this movie is where Marilyn established herself in the lore of Hollywood. The lore of Hollywood as he put it was what this
decade would be how future generations look at these movies. The mere fact
that an unknown actress was being included on a poster promoting a big Hollywood movie of its day, indicates the studio was well aware of how Marilyn
came across on the big screen. One of the biggest movie magazines during
the release of the feature, Photoplay, wrote when reviewing *The Asphalt Jungle*,
"There's a beautiful blonde too, name of Marilyn Monroe, who plays Calhern's girlfriend, and makes the most of her footage". Another strange note
regarding Marilyn and *The Asphalt Jungle* is when she was trying out for the
role which actually called for Marilyn to lie on a couch, Marilyn auditioned
lying on the floor. There were many actresses who were up for the part Marilyn auditioned for, mainly because John Huston was one of Hollywood's foremost directors. He had plenty of great classic movies to his credit. The agents
of all the aspiring actresses always sent their clients to audition for a Huston
production. The list of John Huston's movies before *The Asphalt Jungle*, included *The Maltese Falcon*, (1941), *The Treasure of the Sierra Madre*, (1948), and
Key Largo (1948). It can be noted that all of those movies are on the AFI's
list of the greatest movies of all time. Marilyn worked hard to prepare for her
audition with this great director. She knew it was a golden opportunity and
she spent almost every possible minute of the three days and nights leading
up to her big day, going over the material. The audition was held in a sound
stage on the MGM lot. Marilyn asked John Huston if she could recline on
the floor for her reading as part of her interpretation of the character, and he
agreed. Afterward, Marilyn requested to do it one more time. Even though
Mr. Huston allowed her another reading, it really wasn't necessary. John Huston confided in friends that he had decided to give her the role following
her first attempt. He also told the media that "Marilyn didn't get the part
because of any outside influences", which was suggested, Huston went on to
say, "She got it because she was damned good". This performance by Marilyn
is extremely important when making the case that Marilyn deserved an Oscar
nomination, at the least. No, her overall performance in *The Asphalt Jungle*, is

by no means Oscar worthy. It is a clear indication of her potential for future roles. Her unique persona was establishing itself. Marilyn and the character she created, Angela Phinlay, are both memorable. That is saying something because, each and every character in *The Asphalt Jungle* demonstrated perfection. John Huston directed each scene as if it were the most important one in the film. This gave every scene its own sense of urgency, of importance, and kept a consistent tone, making the film one long, tragic descent into doom. It is also a testament to Huston's genius as a director, because it was Huston who first utilized Marilyn's image to its best advantage. He was the first director that truly understood the complexity of that image, a unique trait Marilyn had that escaped most directors she worked with.

The Asphalt Jungle is like other Huston's films in that the theme revolves around a group of men in pursuit of a quest that ultimately fails. In some cases like in *The Treasure of the Sierra Madre*, it was greed. But often because a woman lures or distracts the men from their goal, as was the case in *Key Largo* and this crime drama. In *The Asphalt Jungle*, Marilyn's character, Angela Phinlay, isn't a bad girl, regardless, she causes the ruination of the lawyer played by Louis Calhern. His need to hold on to her as though she were a priceless possession, despite the expenses and personal risks involved, results in his downfall. The erotic innocence of Marilyn's image helped her to flesh out Angela and make her real. The girl is never painted as conniving or calculating, yet the lawyer's obsession for her is no less believable. Both John Huston and Marilyn made sure when she was in a scene, you the viewer were getting 100% from each of them. A good example is when Marilyn opens a door preceded by loud knocking. What follows is a spontaneous dialog from Marilyn, "Haven't you bothered me enough, you big banana head? Just try breaking my door". However no matter how many times you watch that short scene you will agree, there is Marilyn, sultry, innocent, glamorous unlike any actress before or since. It is all and only Marilyn. The main reason for mentioning such a brief moment from a forgotten movie classic is because this movie was unique. Try to name an actress or an actor whose performance in *The Asphalt Jungle* is the best, you will not. For sure you will like them all.

The New York Post wrote in their movie review, It is the crime drama of the decade, and it may be the best one ever made. The New York Times wrote, "Everyone in the picture, gives an unimpeachable performance".

Another one of the award winning box office hit movies of the 1950's was *All About Eve*. This movie was a very expensive production with many of Hollywood's top stars. Marilyn's role was slightly smaller than her previous one in *The Asphalt Jungle*. The role that Marilyn had however, was pivotal to the narrative of *All About Eve*. In this drama Marilyn's character, Miss Caswell, was in fact a very shallow individual who had absolutely no pretense about using her beauty and her body to get a break in the theater. As you can well imagine Marilyn was more than suited for this type of role and was by far the most glamorous star in the entire production. Miss Caswell provides a counterpoint to the more cunning Eve, played by the seasoned actress, Anne Baxter, who uses underhanded tricks to get to the top. After Eve is exposed for the cruel manipulator that she is, Miss Caswell's more obvious methods are seen as almost honest in comparison. The rest of the cast of *All About Eve*, both male and female was an impressive one and featured, Anne Baxter, Bette Davis, Celeste Holm, Thelma Ritter and George Sanders. To confirm how good *All About Eve* was, all four of the female stars, received Academy Award nominations. Both Anne Baxter and Bette Davis were nominated for best actress and Celeste Holm and Thelma Ritter for best supporting actress. George Sanders won the Oscar for best supporting actor and the motion picture was the winner of the Oscar for Best Picture of the Year. The director, Joseph L. Mankiewicz won the Oscar in the Best Director category. This was a movie that has been revered as a cinematic gem, with outstanding award winning performances. It also made over 122 million dollars at the box office. Marilyn it seemed, was never in awe of these major actors and exactly as Marilyn had done in *The Asphalt Jungle*, she made a strong impression as Miss Caswell. When you are cast as a relative unknown in a motion picture that receives more Academy Award nominations than any motion picture in the

entire decade to follow, then you make everyone take notice, you are unique. Even the great Bette Davis was somewhat taken back by Marilyn. So much so that in one rather small scene she shared with this relative unknown, the following transpired. Bette Davis saw the rushes of the scene in particular and wanted the scene to be shot over. She said to the director, "Okay, we need to re-shoot, and you need to move her, (Marilyn), out of the center of the frame, because no one will listen to a word I'm saying as long as that creature is sharing the screen with me". The great Bette Davis knew! Marilyn was so outstanding in her performance that Twentieth Century-Fox decided to give her another screen test. It was not often during this era of Hollywood that actors or actresses were given additional screen tests, there were no second chances. Marilyn Monroe had proved to everyone on numerous occasions that it was her acting, her delivery, her aura that she always projected was special. It proved to be an accurate description because it made the studio take notice time and time again. Now with these very impressive performances, Marilyn returned to the sound stages of Twentieth Century-Fox for her second screen test. This time the test was done with sound, unlike her previous one, and this time Marilyn was given a scene to do with another actor. The scene involved a dispute between a gangster and his girlfriend, and the gangster was none other then one of Hollywood's best film noir actors of his day. The actor was Richard Conte, and could he act, and boy was he tough on Marilyn. Many years later Richard Conte recalled the screen test with great detail and how he admired Marilyn. He stated that she was very intense during that screen test and it was her intensity, her total concentration of being a serious actress that impressed him. He also went on to say that her acting style looked quite natural on screen, even though it was her beauty that always was the first thing that the audience saw. Well the screen test was so good that Darryl F. Zanuck, the head of Twentieth Century-Fox, signed Marilyn to her second contract with the studio, another rare occasion. There were two very promising incidents right around this time that really helped get Marilyn Monroe the national and world attention she deserved. The first was that Marilyn was featured in Life magazine in a full color spread, a major accomplishment for any star in Hollywood during that era. Only a few special Hollywood stars would get the distinction of being featured in a full color layout in America's favorite magazine. Then it was announced that Marilyn was going to be a presenter at the Academy Award ceremony, an even bigger way for Marilyn to get additional exposure. Marilyn was beaming when she received the official notice. She was even able to select a dress from the 20th Century Fox wardrobe department where she was employed at the time. It was not an easy task, because as one might imagine there were literally thousands of magnificent dresses to choose from. There were many unique and one of a kind period dresses from some of the historical movies that 20th Century Fox was famous for. The dress that Marilyn Monroe finally selected was without a doubt made for her. It was a cloud of black tulle and now Marilyn was more than ready to make her appearance at the 23rd Annual Academy Awards. Of special note according to Made for Each Other: Fashion and the Academy Awards, moments before presenting the sound-recording award, Marilyn discovered a tear in her dress and insisted, "I can't go on!". The skirt was mended backstage and she was able to make what would be her only Oscar appearance. The reason why Marilyn was even considered as a presenter was, most likely due to her appearance in *All About Eve*, which was by far one of best motion pictures of the previous year. Marilyn was chosen to present the Oscar for outstanding achievement in sound recording to Thomas T. Moulton for his work on *All About Eve*. The exposure at the Oscars paid off in big dividends and Marilyn was very surprised that she had so many fans. Right about this time she managed to get more fan mail than, Elizabeth Taylor, Lana Turner, Katherine Hepburn, Grace Kelly, Audrey Hepburn, Bette Davis, and Natalie Wood. Fan Mail was a very big deal during the Golden Age of Hollywood and almost every movie fan always took the time to request a photo or even an autograph from their favorite stars. The way the process worked was, if for instance you were a fan of Errol Flynn or Lana Turner, all you had to do was send a letter to their respective studio, mention that you would like a photograph of that star and in return for your request you would receive a nice photo. In some cases

the glossy 8X10 might even include a hand written autograph. The studios had their own publicity department dedicated to this process. 20th Century Fox studio was overwhelmed with requests for photos of Marilyn and when those requests became significantly much more than any of the other 20th Century Fox stars, the studio head, Darryl F. Zanuck became suspicious and felt that it was a friend of Marilyn who was manipulating the totals from within the studio. After an investigation by Mr. Zanuck and his staff the determination was made that the public were truly enamored with his star and not some internal feat of espionage. Hollywood was filled with really big named actresses during this era and for Marilyn to get such an unbelievable amount of fan mail was a major accomplishment. The list of female stars during that time is a virtual who's who of some of the greatest actresses in Hollywood. It was apparent that Zanuck would now find movies where he could place her to promote his B-movie fare. It was sort of a slap in the face mentality for Marilyn to be considered as merely a B-movie actress. As fate would have it the only positive development that came out of Mr. Zanuck's decision was the popularity of Marilyn grew by leaps and bounds. From a business decision standpoint Zanuck's studio did actually turn great profits from the next group of light hearted comedies that Marilyn Monroe was cast in. These movies were put together with a very limited budget and Marilyn really didn't have much of a role in any of them. In reality it can be said they were merely variations of the role that made Zanuck aware that he had a star, Marilyn's depiction of Miss Caswell in *All About Eve*. One of these B-movie comedies, *As Young As You Feel* got the attention of the critics and Marilyn was praised for her short, but impressive performance. It was apparent that there was a lot more underneath this glamorous new movie star. If you are able to track down these early movies that Marilyn was cast in merely as an extra you will agree that Marilyn Monroe still stands out from the other actors and actresses.

CHAPTER 3

The 1950s:
Evolution of Perfection

"Someone said to me, "If fifty percent of the experts in Hollywood said you had no talent and should give up, what would you do? My answer was then and still is, if a hundred percent told me that, all one hundred percent would be wrong."

IN THE DECADE OF THE 1950's Marilyn Monroe was cast in many movies, but in 1952 Marilyn was featured in five productions. These movies were all B-movies exactly the type of movies that Darryl F. Zanuck, the head of 20th Century Fox Studios, had in mind after Marilyn's second screen test. In light of his investigation relative to the unusual amount of fan mail that Marilyn was receiving, turning out to be a fan phenomenon, the cameras were ready to roll. These movies were all made on a rather limited budget and produced in a very short shooting schedule. Mr. Zanuck first and foremost was a business man and he knew he had a star in Marilyn, a commodity that would certainly

With Dan Dailey in *A Ticket to Tomahawk* (1950)

A Ticket to Tomahawk (1950)

Cast of *A Ticket to Tomahawk* (1950)

bring in plenty of cash. It would be one of the very first times in his studio's history that his B-movies would be featuring a star that guaranteed box office revenue. Mr. Zanuck knew there was something special about the way the public was gravitating towards Marilyn. She had something special. That something special was going to be put up on the big screen for the movie going public to see, more and more of Marilyn. This segment of her film career I consider as her development period. It was a time when if she had the opportunity to star in some of the Hollywood classics of the 1950's and maybe, just maybe, she might have generated an Oscar buzz. There were a

All About Eve with Bette Davis and George Sanders (1950)

couple of juicy roles that were so good any female lead would get noticed and their female stars should be nominated for an Oscar. That's show business as they say. One movie in particular that really stands out and a role that Marilyn could have easily fit the part for was, *The Bad and the Beautiful*, which actually won a supporting actress Oscar for its star, Gloria Grahame. It was a unique movie for its time and the MGM studio where it was produced, made sure

As Young as You Feel with Wally Brown (1951)

the script would garnish many awards by loading up the cast with Hollywood heavyweights. The movie was so good that even today it holds the record for winning five Oscars, even though it was not nominated for best picture. Gloria Grahame had quite a group to work with. The rest of the cast included several movie legends such as Lana Turner, Kirk Douglas, Walter Pidgeon, Dick Powell, Barry Sullivan, Leo G. Carroll and Gilbert Roland. Try to visualize a major motion picture with both Marilyn Monroe and Lana Turner vying for your attention. The role that enabled Gloria Grahame to bring home the Oscar in *The Bad and the Beautiful* was perfect for Marilyn. That role was about a southern belle, Gloria, who was married to Dick Powell, a college professor who had written a book that Kirk Douglas, a Hollywood director, wants to make. There are many sub-plots involving all the stars such as Lana Turner's character as a washed up alcoholic actress. Most of the better scenes are told in flashbacks. Marilyn as the southern belle wife would have been spectacular. The role called for the character of the wife of the writer to fall in love with Gilbert Roland, an actor friend of Kirk Douglas, but they are both killed in a plane crash as they are running away after falling deeply in love. Marilyn, in a strange coincidence shared many of Gloria Grahame's off screen problems, most notably numerous troubled relationships which were common in both actresses. Gloria Grahame also had four failed marriages, while Marilyn had three. It is fate that sometimes plays a major role in life, and of course, Hollywood success. Had Marilyn Monroe been working for MGM and was cast in *The Bad and the Beautiful*, it can be said that she would have at the least been nominated for an Oscar. Another movie role of the year 1952 that created an Oscar nomination for best supporting actress was in the movie, *Moulin Rouge*. One of the stars was a virtual newcomer, Colette Marchand, and she garnered the nomination for her portrayal of a Paris streetwalker who is rescued from the police by the character of Toulouse-Lautrec, played by Jose Fererr. He was also nominated for an Oscar as best actor, but lost out to Gary Cooper in *High Noon*. The movie, *Moulin Rouge* was also nominated for the best picture Oscar, but it too lost to *High Noon*. Marilyn could have easily slipped into the role of Marie Charlet, the character that Colette Marchand received such rave reviews for and eventually the Oscar nomination. Colette never came close to duplicating her Oscar nominated role and after only three additional movie roles she never appeared in films again. Another interesting twist of fate regarding *Moulin Rouge*, is the fact that its director was one of Marilyn's early admirers, John Huston. The movie was not made in the United States, but was a European Production made in

Shepperton Studios, Surrey, England. It would have been difficult for John Huston to get Marilyn released from 20th Century Fox Studios on loan as was common place during the decade of the 1950's, but it sure is a case for conjecture. Meanwhile, Marilyn Monroe was relegated to movies in 1952 with the following titles, *Clash by Night, We're Not Married, Don't Bother to Knock, Monkey Business*, and a segment in O. *Henry's Full House*. There are some very interesting facts about these movies that need to be looked at a little closer, when making the argument of how Hollywood perceived their

With Alan Hale in *Hometown Story* (1951)

biggest female star. Over the years, since we lost Marilyn Monroe at such a very young age, many lists of her movies and her the rating of her acting ability have been compiled. For example, the list of Marilyn's biggest grossing

Let's Make it Legal with Claudette Colbert and Macdonald Carey (1951)

Love Nest (1951)

Scudda Hoo! Scadda Hay!

movies has ten of her movies listed, but not even one of the five movies made in the year 1952 is on the list. By stark contrast, three of the movies that Marilyn made in 1952 are on the top ten list ranked by her fans. The movies came in at a ranking of number 8, *Clash By Night*, number 9, *Don't Bother to Knock*, and number 10, *Monkey Business*. Another interesting fact when looking at this list is that movie number 1 was, *All About Eve*, the very first movie that actually made everyone aware of her presence. This movie enabled Marilyn to get another contract at 20th Century Fox. *All About Eve* beat out the number 2 movie on the list, *Some Like it Hot*, which most people believe is by far Marilyn's best overall performance. Upon taking a closer look of those three Marilyn Monroe movies of 1952 that did make it to a critically acclaimed list, some interesting arguments can be made. When you consider an actress or actors overall talent relative to just how good they are, and more importantly does this individual deserve an award for his or her performance, many factors come into play. The most important was the overall quality of

the interpretation of the character, someone who was believable, interesting and unique. Marilyn most definitely had the ability to interpret all her roles with professionalism. The performances all came across completely natural. Her screen persona also contained a unique underlying quality of innocence. There are many stories and myths surrounding Marilyn, more than any other actress can lay claim to, even by today's standards. When you consider that she was only thirty-six years old when she died, the magnitude of myths associated with her, is truly astounding. Words cannot describe what Marilyn had, it was unique and never duplicated. The only way to say it, was saying she had the "it" factor. It certainly was much more than looks or appearance

O. Henry's Full House with Charles Laughton (1952)

and this little true story will help explain what that something was, if at all possible. Marilyn loved New York City, she even mentioned she would love to live in Brooklyn. Well, one day at the height of her career when it was virtually impossible for any star of her magnitude to go out in public without

Clash by Night (1952)

being mobbed the following took place. Marilyn was walking in the heart of New York City with a friend. The only disguise, if you want to call it that, was a pair of oversized sunglasses and a coat. Marilyn was enjoying the fact that she was completely incognito. She was a massive star at the time and nobody was even giving her a second glance. On this occasion Marilyn was perhaps just another plain old New Yorker. This is an indication that she had that ability to turn off "that thing" that happened when the camera was on her. The friend was amazed at how they were able to enjoy this anonymity and remarked, "It's so weird how nobody is looking at you". The friend realized the glasses and the coat were not much of a disguise. Marilyn grinned slyly and said, "Do you want to see her?". By "her" she was referring to herself in the third person. The friend said yes. In an instant Marilyn took off the glasses. It seemed like all she did was make a slight adjustment in her face and something magical happened. However, the magic and transformation came from the inside, not the outside. It was not only the face or the body that attracted people to her, it was "that thing". Suddenly passersby started to gather and stare, and within a few short minutes Marilyn was surrounded by a crowd of autograph hounds. It's the fact that she was able to turn it on from the inside and didn't rely on costumes or only her looks. That was the real genius of Marilyn Monroe, her unique persona. While this interesting story is being retold, it is another indication of how unique Marilyn Monroe really was. Try to find a really bad photograph, you will not. In regard to Marilyn spending time in New York she was one of the only big stars who could walk Broadway, Times Square incognito.

The year was 1953 and for some reason it was one of those years that in terms of Hollywood releases, it was a magical year. It was a year that if you were a movie buff, you found yourself having a multitude of choices of movies to see. Television was not a major part of society's leisure time, and the movie theaters were where most people spent their money for entertainment. The list of classic and iconic movies released in 1953 is perhaps one of greatest of the entire decade. Some of the most memorable ones were, *From Here To Eternity*, which won a record eight Oscars, *The Robe, Stalag 17, Julius Ceasar, Roman Holiday*, and *Lily*. There was a pair of unique westerns, *Shane*, with Alan Ladd and *Hondo*, with John Wayne. Once again science fiction and horror movies made noise at the box office with such classics as, H.G. Wells'

The War of The Worlds, It Came From Outer Space, House of Wax and *Invaders from Mars*. Marlon Brando had a big hit movie in, *The Wild One*, while Tony Curtis wowed audiences in *Houdini*. *Stalag 17* had no less than three Oscar nominations, William Holden for Best Actor, Robert Strauss for Best Supporting Actor and Billy Wilder for Best Director. *Mogambo* had some Hollywood heavyweight actresses in its cast. Both Ava Gardner, nominated for Best Actress and Grace Kelly, nominated for Best Supporting Actress failed to walk away with Oscars. Walt Disney made his mark in 1953 with one of his classic animation feature films, *Peter Pan*. There were plenty of top flight musicals including, *Kiss Me Kate, The Band Wagon* with Fred Astaire and *Calamity Jane* with Doris Day. Marilyn Monroe was also busy in 1953, she starred in a musical, *Gentlemen Prefer Blondes*, a comedy *How to Marry a Millionaire*, and a film-noir drama, *Niagara*. It was the first movie released in 1953 that had Marilyn Monroe as its star. Of course 20th Century Fox Studio promoted the movie with advertisements, which were the main promotional materials in the 50's. Dynamic color posters and full page ads in magazines featured a very seductive Marilyn with *Niagara Falls* as a backdrop. When the movie was released it was hailed as being a tight film noir drama, even though it was filmed in color. Film noir movies were for the most part always shot in black and white which added to the melodrama. Marilyn Monroe handled the role of a cheating wife with an air of innocence, that when you watch the movie comes across quite well. During this time of her career, unlike what most people thought, Marilyn was studying her craft and wanted to evolve in a serious actress. Most of Marilyn's previous roles were in light comedies. There is a scene with wet asphalt in the early morning light that is an indication that the director was striving for a dynamic location more than the use of just his cast. Marilyn handled the swirling waters, the mist, cascading roar of the falls with her contrasting demure nature. It was perhaps one of Marilyn's greatest dramatic performances, having to compete with not only others in the cast, but the outstanding location shots. When you view the movie you will fully realize this fact and appreciate the underlying talent Marilyn had. If you have never seen this classic, please make sure to pick a

night where you can give the movie your undivided attention. It can even
be a rainy Saturday afternoon. Marilyn will engulf you with her captivating
and demure performance. This movie, is one of those special movies where
the character she portrays will come across as a real person, perhaps one you
might have crossed paths with. *Niagara* is really a timeless classic and its
story, though not a unique one, will capture the relevance it had decades ago.
One of the surprising elements is a plot twist that she handles with a style
and grace that is missing from today's productions. Marilyn for certain would
have handled similar roles with the professionalism she conveyed in *Niagara*,
her first real dramatic role. Two years later a very controversial movie, *Baby
Doll*, would have been another vehicle for Marilyn, to get a nomination for.
The movie went on to secure an academy award nomination for Carroll Baker,
but she lost to Ingrid Bergman who won for her role in *Anastasia*. *Baby Doll*
might have been the perfect role in 1956 for Marilyn who was close to the age
of its star, Carroll Baker. The role was of a 19 year old wild, blonde teenager.
The additional seductive aura that Marilyn was able to turn on without trying,
would have certainly received rave reviews and of course the nomination.

The studio tried to get the most out of their star and Marilyn's next
movie was *Gentlemen Prefer Blondes*. The studio head Darryl F. Zanuck
wanted his star, Marilyn to show off her talents in a big production musical.
Zanuck knew it was a time that the movie going public would much rather
see Marilyn dancing and singing in fancy costumes, than using her in some
melodrama. Gentlemen Prefer Blondes featured another one of 20th Century
Fox's top actresses, Jane Russell, who at the time was five years older than
Marilyn. The movie was based on the smash Broadway musical, eye popping
costumes and song and dance numbers that translated perfectly on the big
screen. Fresh off the heels of the great dramatic performance in *Niagara*,
Marilyn not only convinces the audience she can star in a big production
musical, but even sing. Her rendition of the classic "Diamonds are a Girl's
Best Friend", remains today as one of the most memorable and iconic songs
of all time. It was a rendition that once you see her performing it, years later
if you hear it on the radio, your mind visualizes Marilyn, looking right at you,

melting your heart. Let's not forget Jane Russell, who was also fantastic in this movie and brought a dynamic presence that was a perfect complement to Marilyn. Many people who saw this movie when it was released over sixty years ago realized that they were viewing a classic movie, but also that they were now instant fans of that girl called Marilyn. They say that when you are rewarded for a performance in a movie, it is not just for the role. They say it requires a total overall performance that has many aspects to it. Marilyn Monroe surely conveyed all of those qualifications and much more. The very first time you see her shuffling along, you feel that boy is that a really dumb blond. That was exactly what Marilyn wanted you to feel. Then as the movie developed she became even more of that dumb blonde character, but you realized it was to win over all the men that were after her. Marilyn was a perfectionist and the one thing that was apparent was that she knew how voluptuous she really was, and her persona popped off the screen. It was almost as if every little movement Marilyn made was directed to you the viewer on a one on one basis that has never been duplicated. Every little pout, every little movement of her body, was just for you. When Marilyn sings, "Diamonds are a Girl's Best Friend", you don't want the song to end. In *Gentlemen Prefer Blondes*, we also get a big dose of Marilyn doing comedy, and it proved to be more than anyone expected. It was a tight, crisp, ultra professional performance that can be said had a bit of perfection attached to it. True, the scenery and the overall color production added to the high quality of the movie, but it was all Marilyn Monroe. She made this movie a classic, one that stands the true test of time and this one really fits that definition, a testimony to Marilyn.

She had one more movie that 20th Century Fox released in that same year, 1953. It was a comedy, *How to Marry a Millionaire*. This third and final film released in 1953 starring Marilyn had quite a seasoned cast. There were two great actresses, Betty Grable and Lauren Bacall. Marilyn had many more male actors in the cast to interact with. There was Rory Calhoun, David Wayne, William Powell, Cameron Mitchell, Alexander D'Arcy, and Fred Clark. She wore glasses for most of the movie and it showed a different side

to her glamorous looks. This movie had a much weaker plot than *Gentlemen Prefer Blondes* and both Lauren Bacall and Betty Grable really didn't fit as close friends with the much younger Marilyn. If you want to make a case for how great an actress Marilyn really was, this movie has to be added to the list, but, it only is important because there was no doubt that Marilyn was going to be a dominant actress in Hollywood. Once again the role and plot really had no relevance, but the studio reaped the benefits. Only two other movies

did better than *Gentlemen Prefer Blondes* at the box office in 1953. Those
two movies were the biblical saga, *The Robe*, and Walt Disney's animation
classic, *Peter Pan*. The studio, 20th Century Fox, was very satisfied with their
blockbuster, *Gentlemen Prefer Blondes* which took in over 213 million dollars.
Darryl F. Zanuck was elated with how his gamble with Marilyn Monroe was
paying off with very big dividends. It would be hard for Mr. Zanuck and his
studio to upset the apple cart and roll the dice again by giving Marilyn roles
that were not commercially profitable.

Don't Bother to Knock with Richard Widmark (1952)

CHAPTER 4

The Missed Opportunities

*"I used to think as I looked at the Hollywood night, there must be
thousands of girls sitting alone like me, dreaming of becoming a movie star,
but I'm not going to worry about them. I'm dreaming the hardest."*

IT WAS A COOL BRISK NIGHT, not really dark yet as the sky was bathed in
various shades of reds, oranges and dark magentas. The sun had already set
and said goodbye once again. As the automobiles took their place in line to
gain entrance to the drive-in, the flashing lights of the marque reflected off
their shiny paint. One of the movies playing was, *There's No Business Like
Show Business*, but its title was overshadowed by the name of its star, Marilyn
Monroe. The year was 1954 and only two movies were released with Marilyn
Monroe in the cast. Having your motion picture being featured at a drive-in
movie venue was not a negative because in the mid 1950's there were over
4000 drive-in movie theaters in the United States. Drive-in movie theaters

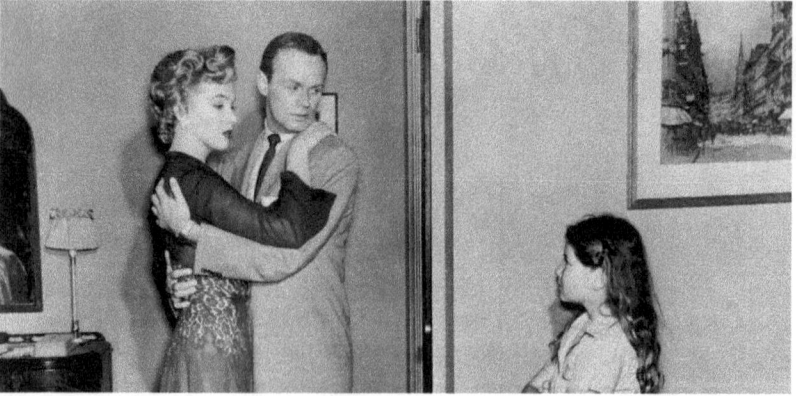

Don't Bother to Knock (1952)

were famous for showing twin-billings and the second feature this particular evening was *Seven Brides For Seven Brothers*. The versatility of Marilyn Monroe was once again showcased in *There's No Business Like Show Business*, a role that had many challenges for Marilyn. It was a role that required her to be a dramatic actress, a comedian, and to perform some musical numbers. The movie also had Marilyn billed opposite many of Hollywood's biggest male stars of the day. Donald O'Connor, Dan Dailey and Hugh O'Brian. When you think of actresses who made a name for themselves in musicals, the two female leads in this movie had all the credentials, but the versatile Ethel Merman and Mitzi Gaynor were actually upstaged by Marilyn's overall performance. It is said that Marilyn Monroe was becoming a smart

We're Not Married with David Wayne (1952)

business woman at this crossroad of her career and even negotiated to be in *There's No Business Like Show Business*, only if she could star in *The Seven Year Itch*. When you consider the list of classic movies that were released in the year 1954 it is another major accomplishment that *There's No Business Like Show Business* beat out many great movies in reviews from the critics. It was Marilyn's performance, as well as, the entire production that all played into the mix. Once again Marilyn was praised for her delivery and considered to be a well rounded addition to the cast. Some of those movies you are familiar

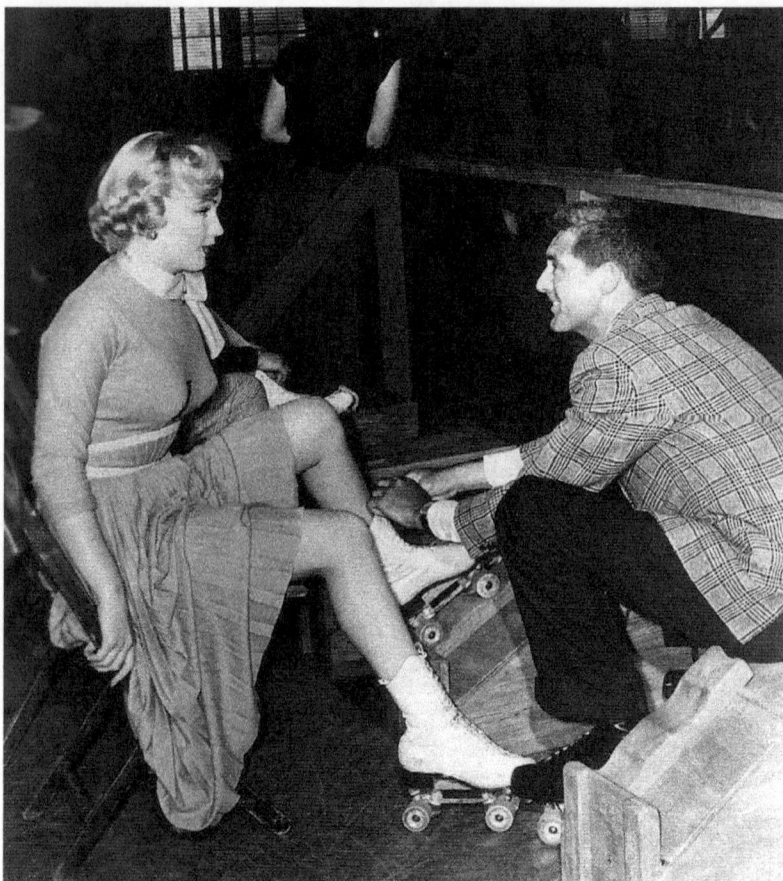

Monkey Business with Cary Grant (1952)

with from 1954 are, *On The Waterfront, White Christmas, The Caine Mutiny, A Star Is Born, Three Coins In the Fountain, The* High *and the Mighty* and *Rear Window*. Most critics went on to say that the most memorable aspects of *There's No Business Like Show Business* was, Marilyn Monroe, now the biggest star in Hollywood at the time. They went on to say Marilyn was clearly in a different league than the rest of the cast in terms of sexuality. Mitzi Gaynor was by no means hard to look at, but an indication of Marilyn's star power involves the song and dance number Heat Wave. The song was supposed to be one of Mitzi Gaynor's tunes, but the studio, most likely coming from Zanuck

Gentlemen Prefer Blondes (1953)

himself, and he decided to give it to Marilyn. It became one of those movie moments that will be forever associated with Marilyn. Another number, "After You Get What You Want", showcased more of Marilyn's persona and even featured one of the many spectacular costumes. She also brought out her tremendous vulnerability that no other comic actress could convey, with believability. She could play wounded characters, perhaps because she was so wounded herself. Watching her character suffer over her love for Tim played by Donald O'Connor while she also wants a successful career is very moving and believable, it most likely bring you to tears. Keep in mind this performance by her is part of her complete body of work and surely in an indication of her overall versatile talent. As the crowd left the huge outdoor parking lot, it was a surrealistic scene with a full moon shining brightly over the huge outdoor movie screen. Bright red lights looked like dots in a long line of cars. Perhaps as I gazed at that moon it was an indication of just how bright Marilyn's star would shine for all time. It was only the second movie with her as its star that I ever saw, but it left the impression with me to want to see every movie Marilyn would make from now on. The studio was a corporation with profits as their ultimate goal. The quality of their movies or the performances of their stars was only measured by box office success. Mr. Zanuck got exactly what he wanted once again from Marilyn. *There's No Business Like Show Business* racked in a sizable 190 million dollars at the box office. It was apparent when it was time for Oscar nominations, why should

Zanuck care if Marilyn was nominated, he already had achieved what he wanted from her just being in his movie, a big paycheck. Chances are, he wanted things to evolve exactly like that. "Show Business" meant big business profits. There was only one other movie that Marilyn Monroe made in the year 1954, *River of No Return*. The versatility of Marilyn Monroe was once again challenged this time in a very dramatic role. It was hard to envision

Marilyn in an action adventure movie. This role had her billed opposite one of Hollywood's biggest male stars of the day, Robert Mitchum. It would be a new experience for Marilyn, because this movie was also

set in several wild outdoor settings. The locations were some of the most beautiful ones in North America, such as Lake Louise in Jasper National Park, and Alberta Canada. It was a unique challenge for Marilyn, not only working side by side with Robert Mitchum, but also the director, Otto Preminger, a consummate director, always expecting nothing but perfection from his stars. Mr. Preminger was not an easy person to get along with on any movie set, much less one with many challenges.

When I got my first glimpse of Marilyn on the big screen it was at the drive-in movie. This second Marilyn Monroe movie encounter was in a very special indoor movie setting. The time in the early days of the motion picture experience was one where the movie business involved many aspects of entertainment, not just buying a ticket at a multi-plex and picking from as many as twenty or more movies to see, as it is today. Back in the days when Marilyn Monroe was a star the movie theaters were all single screen venues and there always was a double feature and in some cases a triple feature showing. This particular afternoon I decided to see a cowboy movie, *Apache*, starring the great Burt Lancaster. It turned out that the second film on the twin bill was a Marilyn Monroe movie, *The River of No Return*. I, like everyone who enjoyed movies and had heard plenty about Marilyn Monroe and was inundated with her image on so many magazines you would have trouble counting them. The poster outside the movie house of *The River of No Return*, was a striking one with of course a river, but the two images of Marilyn is what caught my eye. In one image she was wearing a bathing suit type costume holding a guitar, in the other image she was being held by Robert Mitchum and they were both smiling widely. In those golden years of movies it was always customary to have similar movies on a double bill, two war movies, two horror movies, two comedies, two musicals and in this case two westerns. It is a good time to really set the scene for this movie adventure this cold wintery Saturday in New York City. The neighborhood where I lived had no less than seven movie theaters and some of them could really be considered as movie palaces. The one showing *The River of No Return* was the Loews, 175th Street. What a movie theater to watch my very first Marilyn Monroe movie, even though it was not my reason for going to the movies that day. The Loews 175th Street opened in 1930 and was the third largest in America with a capacity of 3,600 seats. The theater was one of the many stops in New York that was on the 25th Anniversary of the League of Historic American Theaters list. The building was the last of the five "Wonder Theatres" erected between the years of 1925 and 1930. These "Wonder Theatres" were named to honor the fact

that each had a Morton Wonder Organ. There were five Loews' flagship movie palaces which were built in the New York Metropolitan area. Along with the 175th Street Theatre, there was the Loews' Jersey Theatre, in Jersey City, Loews' Kings Theatre, located in Brooklyn, Loews' Paradise Theatre, in The Bronx, (another of my favorite movie houses) and Loews' Valencia Theatre, in Queens, all of which all opened in 1929. The appeal of the "Wonder Theatre" was its spectacular architecture. The exterior facades were decorated in terra-cotta with hints of Art Deco, Egyptian, Aztec, Mayan, Moorish, Oriental and Persian Design. The interior of these massive structures were ornately decorated with filigreed walls and ceilings, illuminated with directional lighting from within and behind walls. The lobby was ornamented much like an Italian palazzo; it featured marble pillars, and even a goldfish pool, carpeted staircases, and tapestries. These theatres were all the home of the now famous and rare original Robert Morton Wonder Organ. The organ with Twin Chambers is seven stories high. The International Theatre Organ Guild Society has restored this instrument, and holds its International conventions and concerts here. The organ is the only such organ, anywhere left in its original site. So it is evident that the movie theater where I got my second

glimpse of Marilyn Monroe on the big screen was almost as big attraction as Marilyn herself. I must admit that the first feature, *Apache*, was a great movie in its own right. Burt Lancaster was just spectacular in the role of a renegade Apache warrior, one of the last of his kind who escapes from capture and returns to his homeland. The movie also featured Jean Peters and a very young, but also dynamic Charles Bronson. The other unique quality of seeing a movie in the mid nineteen fifties was the intermission between features.

It somehow allowed you as a movie patron to stretch out your legs, but also to make a trip to the snack bar. One of my favorite treats were the chocolate covered mini ice cream balls called Bon Bons. This intermission also allowed you to somewhat erase the previous movie and get you set for the next feature. In this case the next feature was billed as an action adventure movie filmed in the savage wilderness, complete with the added feature of Cinemascope. It sounded like a great premise but it was the on screen persona of Marilyn Monroe that truly stole the show. When the movie was made both of Marilyn's male co-stars were the biggest draws in Hollywood. Robert Mitchum and Rory Calhoun usually received top billing and Rory had previously been in a Marilyn feature the previous year, *How to Marry a Millionaire*. The movie was as exciting as the images depicted on the poster. It had plenty of action

and adventure and there were even Indians thrown in for added excitement. Marilyn Monroe was without a doubt the most dynamic actress I had even seen. It was everything about her, and later that evening when I described her to some friends I coined the phrase, "Marilyn was the total package". When she was introduced in the movie she had another attribute that I never expected, she had a really unique and good voice. Marilyn played a dance hall

singer and the musical parts of this particular movie didn't detract from all of the action and adventure I had hoped to see. One of the songs that she sung, the title of the movie, The River of No Return, still sticks in my mind as a very sultry catchy tune. I came out of the theater in awe of Marilyn Monroe. I knew she had made movies in the past but my interest centered on western, horror, sword and sandal movies and of course anything that Errol Flynn starred in. Now I knew I was going to become an avid Marilyn Monroe fan, but I was also going to try and see all her movies that I missed because I really was unaware of her great screen presence. Of note regarding this movie, *The River of No Return*, the director Otto Preminger was very influential in Hollywood and he pulled no punches while relating how Marilyn Monroe was very difficult to work with. It is just another person in power who perhaps insured Marilyn would be looked over when nominations were made. It was a big acting challenge for Marilyn and the action around her truly added to the drama. In one memorable scene Marilyn, Robert Mitchum and Mitchum's son in the movie played by Tommy Rettig, of Lassie fame, are forced to take a dangerous journey down the river on a crude wooden raft. It sets up the interaction between both of these male stars with Marilyn. The interaction is very different because there is drama and a clash of personalities with Robert Mitchum, but Marilyn conveyed a warmth and tenderness with the young star, Rettig that will definitely move you. It was also interesting to see her in a new role somewhat against type, a very resourceful, feisty woman, coupled with emotions. Marilyn really saved the picture from total disaster, because she was so compelling. When I recently watched the DVD for research purposes it was apparent to me there were the beginnings of her Strasberg influence from the Actors Studio. The different styles of acting were already developing for Marilyn and laid the groundwork for Marilyn's best work that she achieved a few years later. It can be said she definitely put in a good, if not great performance, considering the script and the sparks that flew between Marilyn and Otto Preminger. This problem between her and Otto manifested itself as Mr. Preminger walked off the picture and Jean Negulesco had to actually finish the movie.

CHAPTER 5

Errol Flynn
Just Like Marilyn

"Everybody says I can't act. They said the same thing about Elizabeth Taylor.
And they were wrong. She was great in A Place in the Sun. *I'll never get the*
right part, anything I really want. My looks are against me. They're too specific."
—Marilyn

"By instinct I'm an adventurer, by choice I'd like to be a writer,
by pure unadultered luck, I'm an actor."
—Errol

IT CAN BE SAID THAT the great swashbuckling hero, Errol Flynn had a female counterpart, Marilyn Monroe. The main reason for this comparison is based on several unique characteristics that these two charismatic movie stars shared. First and foremost was there voracious desire to be with the opposite sex. Both were linked with literally hundreds of romantic partners throughout their short but interesting careers. It can also be noted that strange as it seems they were both married three times, but all of the marriages never lasted. One can only wonder what kind of relationship Marilyn Monroe would have had with Errol Flynn? The second characteristic that they both shared dealt with how the two approached their careers as actors in Hollywood's Golden Age. It was a special time when the stars were always much bigger and important then the movies they starred in. Your average movie patron was attracted to the stars of the movie that he or she decided to attend. If you make a comparison between all of the movies that both Errol Flynn and Marilyn Monroe starred in with most of the movies released today there are also very unique differences. The movies of today rely on special effects and big budgets, coupled with millions of dollars in promotion. These current releases seldom rely on a complex script and are really not entertaining. The performances turned in by the stars of today are convoluted and contrived. If you evaluate the majority of the movies that Errol Flynn and Marilyn Monroe were in, almost all had a dynamic script and the only promotion the movies had were trailers in the theaters and print advertisements. Looking at the cost of promotion in the Golden Age of Hollywood as compared to today the difference is in the tens of millions of dollars. Most of the movies that would not be considered as blockbuster movies by today's standards always were box office hits because of who starred in them and the complexity of the script. These movies could be about virtually any subject, any genre but they had "stars" in the cast. Today the movies that 90% of the time make the top ten list at the box office each weekend most likely have some sort of CGI in their subject matter, and they are productions that are finished in a matter of weeks. In the days when a western made its debut, you could find such big names such as Errol Flynn, Bogart, Cagney, Quinn and Heston in the cast. The western would most likely be a drama that relied heavily on its story and characters. They were always entertaining. That level of entertainment came from the presence of the big name stars who were in the cast. Errol Flynn made a lot of these movies and from a box office standpoint they were always very successful because of the name Errol Flynn in the cast. The same can be said of Marilyn, she was an instant box office draw. When the movies that Marilyn Monroe and Errol Flynn were being produced the way they approached their job, if you want to call it a job, was a mirror image. Errol

Flynn on numerous occasions would decide he wanted to sail the Caribbean in one of his yachts. The problem with his decision was he made the choice while he was in the very middle of starring in a movie. The 1950's were light years away from the internet, cell phones and there was virtually no way to reach anyone who was somewhere docked off shore in a tropical paradise. To make matters worse for Errol Flynn's studio, Warner Brothers, when he returned to the site of the film shoot Errol Flynn would go right back on his yacht. He probably didn't plan it that way but he was a free spirit. If he felt the admonishment from one of the Warner brothers was too harsh, he would not argue, with the Warner in question. Errol would simply smile and give a wave of his hand and off he was, again. It was not unusual for one of Errol Flynn's productions to be shut down for months and not days because of his seafaring ways, and a cavalier attitude. Marilyn Monroe didn't have any yacht to take her away from a movie set, Marilyn decided on her own terms what being late was all about. When Marilyn first entered the movie business she was always very dependable,

always on time for set rehearsals, and studied her lines meticulously. True in the early part of her movie career those lines were few and far between, but she was extremely dedicated and a perfectionist. In some cases Marilyn was merely a walk on, but made sure that walk on part would be noticed. The bigger Marilyn's star power grew the more her habit of being late on the set or not showing up at all most likely infuriated the producers and directors she was working with immensely. This habit contributed to the fact that when it was time for the ballots to be cast for an Academy Award, Marilyn Monroe's name was always omitted, as was the case in Errol Flynn. One of the most

famous confirmations of the fact that everyone connected to the production of a movie in Hollywood knew how widespread Marilyn's lateness was, surfaced at a most prominent place. The event was in New York City at Madison Square Garden, it was a birthday celebration for the then President of the United States, John F. Kennedy. Peter Lawford was the master of ceremonies and as Marilyn Monroe made her way to the microphone to sing happy birthday to the President, Mr. Lawford introduced her as "the late Marilyn Monroe." There were many more similarities but another hard to debate trait that both Errol Flynn and Marilyn Monroe shared was there on screen presence. Of course during the era when they were making movies Hollywood was full of many glamorous movie actresses and handsome leading men. The differences that set the both of them apart from all of the others was a unique and electrifying persona that seemed to jump at you from the screen. It didn't matter what role either of them was cast in or who was their co-star, Errol Flynn and Marilyn Monroe both literally lit up the screen. That quality that they both possessed was present in both of their careers the very first time you saw them, the very first time. The following list of movies that they are famous for, movies that are on everyone's list of the greatest of all time. These movies are just a sampling of some of the two stars best and memorable performances. First, we have Marilyn's Oscar worthy performance that should have at least been nominated. *Some Like it Hot*, how did she get overlooked. The movie is considered the best comedy of all time.

Then in *The Seven Year Itch*, she turned in a performance that was before its time. Marilyn was what made the movie a classic, and she was listed in the credits as The Girl. The skirt scene in The *Seven Year Itch* is Hollywood's number one memorable scene of all time. The image of Marilyn, the skirt blowing in the wind has even been immortalized by a 36 foot steel statue. *The Misfits*, a movie that showed how Marilyn could play opposite Hollywood's

biggest male star, Clark Gable and equal him in her performance. *Gentlemen Prefer Blondes*, she could dance, she could act she could sing. Her "Diamonds are a Girl's Best Friend" rendition in that movie is one that everyone remembers. *Bus Stop*, a great dramatic performance with songs included. In addition some memorable minor and not so minor roles that formulated her style of acting. That list of movies includes *All About Eve, The Asphalt Jungle, Niagara,* and even *The River of No Return.* As far as Errol Flynn goes, *The Adventures of Robin Hood,* is the greatest action adventure movie of all time. A bold statement but Errol was able to create a Robin Hood that was pure perfection. The way he talked, the way he fought, the way he made you believe you were watching Robin Hood. His pirate sagas are unequaled in the characters he portrayed. *Captain Blood*, made him an instant Hollywood idol, his very first starring role. Then his role in *The Sea Hawk* most likely is responsible for getting him named the number one movie pirate of all time. He even beat out Captain Jack Sparrow to get that honor. In *They Died With Their Boots On*, Errol's portrayal of Custer will not only bring you excitement but in one memorable scene, to tears. He proved he could play any historical character with believability. In *Gentleman Jim*, Errol became Jim Corbett right before your eyes. He was the classic hero in *The Charge of the Light Brigade.* Even at the end of his short career, Errol gave what everyone thought was another award winning performance. This time In *The Sun Also Rises*, a movie that allowed Errol to play a character that was close to what he had become. In between Errol made many memorable cowboy movies, such as *Rocky Mountain, Montana, Virginia City, San Antonio, Silver River, Santa Fe Trail* and *Dodge City*. Some of the war movies that Errol starred in were, *Dive Bomber, The Dawn Patrol, Edge of Darkness,* and *Northern Pursuit.* If you have seen any of these movies you already know that Errol like Marilyn has been overlooked for his contribution to Hollywood. It really didn't matter what role they had, they made you feel you had witnessed something special. Each star in their own right has remained a timeless reminder of some day or night you spent watching them in amazement. They both truly left you the viewer with something unique, so unique that you wanted to see them

again, you had to see them again. They had a magical quality that has never been duplicated, a quality that has withstood the test of time and is alluring to the audience today just as it was over fifty or sixty years ago. It is just a mere evaluation but when you are universally thought of in the manner of being iconic while you are still alive. Alive and making movies a slight air of jealousy might have accounted for neither star getting recognized for their on screen accomplishments. Both Errol Flynn and Marilyn Monroe had their share of off screen scandals and most certainly it too played a most important

role in the fact that Hollywood choose to always omit their names when the Academy Awards were being nominated. They were truly the most beautiful and interesting Hollywood actors of all time, who could act, love and live life to the fullest. Marilyn Monroe and Errol Flynn....it is beauty that captures your attention, but personality that captures your heart.

The following is a special tribute that was made about Errol Flynn after he died. It was made by a man who was one of Hollywood's most influential studio heads of all time. The statement of course was meant to describe Errol Flynn, but it is evident it can be used to describe his female counterpart, Marilyn Monroe also.

Jack L. Warner, head of the iconic Warner Brothers studios, on remembering Errol, Jack said it best, "Let's remember him for the good years! When you see a meteor stab the sky, or a bomb explode, or a fire sweep across a dry hillside, the picture is vivid and remains in your mind. So it was with

Errol....he was all the heroes in one magnificent, sexy, animal package....he showered an audience with sparks when he laughed, when he fought, or when he loved. I just wish we had someone around today half as good as Flynn."

Errol Flynn in *Northern Pursuit* (1943)

CHAPTER 6

Academy Award
Misery Loves Company

"Success makes so many people hate you. I wish it wasn't that way. It would be wonderful to enjoy success without envy in the eyes of those around you."

IT SEEMS THAT THE ACADEMY of Motion Picture Arts and Sciences has made a practice of not recognizing some of Hollywood's greatest actors, actresses and even producers and directors. Of course everyone most definitely has different and varied tastes when it comes to not only what they feel are great movies but also great performances by their favorite actor or actress. One of the problems is when a movie or a performance is evaluated by the critics, their critique holds no weight in the nomination process. They, the critics are for the most part are not the ones who cast the ballots for Oscar nominations. Some individuals in Hollywood, writers in particular felt it was the studio heads as well as the agents who were behind the nomination

process. In reality it is a process that has remained secretive for decades, only known to those who have a need to know. This sounds like some plot for a good espionage movie or crime drama, but it is a most important part of Hollywood's mystique. The Academy of Arts and Sciences state that actors nominate actors, directors nominate directors and everyone nominates movies. Add to these facts that in conjunction with the critics' views, the majority of the movie going public also agree that the movie or performance in question is deserving of at the least a nomination. In the case of Marilyn Monroe there have been far too many of Marilyn's performances that truly fit that category. The arguments against her have always been related to her

personality and demeanor involving multiple on-set problems. Today what really matters is how Marilyn Monroe's performance stand up against her critics, and were there other reasons why Marilyn Monroe and countless other movie stars were also completely overlooked. There have been far too many of these so called snubs by the Academy of Motion Picture Arts and Sciences for them to be a coincidence and many have nothing to do with the quality of the movie or performance. It is unfortunate that even the name of the organization that is representing the motion picture industry contains a contradiction, the word Sciences infers a scientific analysis. However there is much more of a personal view and individual opinions that drive the nominating and voting process. Even in the golden years of Hollywood the Oscars were becoming a popularity contest and if you as an actor, actress or producer or director stepped on the wrong toes, it was evident you had no chance of even getting nominated, and a win of the cherished Oscar was completely out of the question. Most if not all of the iconic stars of the golden years of Hollywood are long since gone but the legacy they left behind is in many cases a sad one when you realize how they were never afforded the opportunity to stand before their peers and receive the accolades they deserved. The names read like a list of the greatest stars that ever graced the

motion picture screen, and when you peruse though the list I am certain you will be shocked at the names that appear on it. Your first impression will most definitely be, "I always was sure that he or she got an Oscar for...." That's right it is a very sad part of Hollywood that until now is buried in the past but needs to be addressed for the sake of what these individuals gave to the industry that has evolved into a medium that produces inferior products that will never be able to compare to the art form that bears its name. If those actors and actresses were here today I am certain that they would all have stories of how disappointed they were and how difficult it was to keep their feeling locked up inside when the nominations were read year after year and

they were overlooked. Everyone who prides themselves and the work that they do wants a so called pat on the back, and in the case of the Oscars that "pat" meant not only more starring roles but ones that were sought after by their peers. There was also another factor that most definitely played a part in who was going to get the nomination, that factor had to do with the studio heads. Every studio was led by unique personalities that brought to their corporation a style of management that could virtually make or break a career. The ones that come to mind are Warner Brothers Studios, managed by four head strong brothers, Jack, Harry, Sam and Albert. It was no secret they were not happy with one of their biggest stars, Errol Flynn. Even though Errol Flynn was the biggest money making machine for Warner Brothers Studio for almost a decade, all of the brothers really didn't like his antics off the movie set. Many other studios wanted to borrow, so to speak, Errol for some roles that were tailor made for an actor of his caliber but the Warners always said absolutely not. Their roles were ones that perhaps would get the actor who portrayed them a nod for an Oscar nomination and that was the very last thing that Jack Warner in particular wanted for Errol. It is ironic that one of

Jack Warner's quotes relative to Errol Flynn actually is a testimony of the complete opposite of how Jack Warner treated and spoke of Errol as a person. Jack once said, "When you see a meteor stab the sky, or a bomb explode, or a fire sweep across a dry hillside, the picture is vivid and remains in your mind. So it was with Errol....he was all the heroes in one magnificent, sexy, animal package....he hovered an audience with sparks when he laughed, when he fought, or when he loved. I just wish we had someone around today half as good as Flynn". The Warner Brothers were wired in to the Academy and when it came time for the ballots it was almost a certainty that Jack in

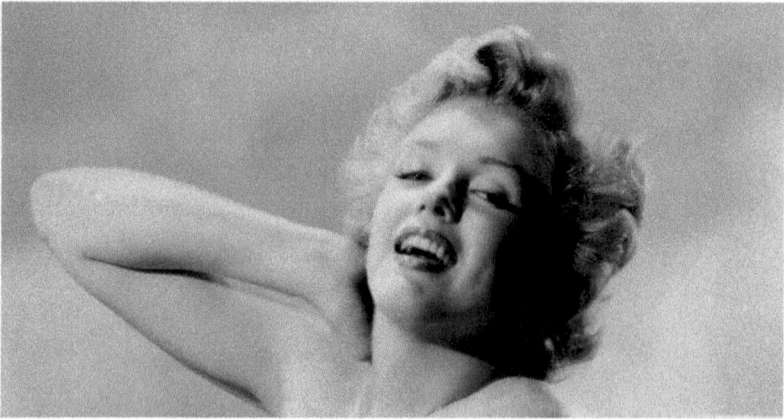

particular made sure Errol's name was always omitted, even though he lamented in the previous quote of a spectacular motion picture actor. Another major studio was Metro-Goldwyn-Mayer, commonly known as MGM and was once the largest and most glamorous of film studios, MGM was founded in 1924 when the entertainment entrepreneur Marcus Loew acquired three other production companies, Metro Pictures, Louis B Mayer Pictures and Goldwyn Pictures Corporation. The name Loew most certainly will come to mind because it was Marcus Loew who owned Loew's movie theaters. His studio MGM also had a stable of iconic actors and actresses and unfortunately Mr Loew never go to see how big his studio, MGM would become because in 1927 only three years after he formed MGM, Marcus died of a heart attack. His studio was evolving into one of the biggest and after his death control of Loew's passed to Nicholas Schenck. It was no secret that may people including Louis B. Mayer referred to him as "Mr. Skunk." He was just one more studio head who was instrumental in who was nominated for Oscars. Another one of the five big original motion picture studios was RKO, Radio-Keith-Orpheum Pictures which not only produced movies but also distributed them. The studio was formed after the Keith-Albee-Orpheum also known as the KAO theater chain and Joseph Kennedy's FBO studio were acquired by RCA in 1928. The then head of RCA, David Sarnoff completed the merger and twenty years later Howard Hughes took over

RKO. Some of the many highlights included the release of *King Kong* in 1933, numerous Fred Astaire and Ginger Rogers musicals and of course *Citizen Kane* in 1941. Even though Citizen Kane is still regarded as the greatest movie of all time, Orson Welles in the title role was nominated for best actor but lost to Gary Cooper in *Sergeant York*. *Citizen Kane* lost to *How Green was My Valley* in the best picture category. Some of the other studios who were also guilty of playing favorites when it came to the Oscars were, Universal Studios and Columbia pictures. In some unique movie history it can be noted that not one but three of Universal Studios films have the distinction of being the highest grossing film upon its release. The unusual fact relative to all three of the films is not one of them was awarded the best

picture Oscar and only two of the three were even nominated. *Jaws* and *E.T. The Extra Terrestrial* were both nominated for best picture but the third film, *Jurassic Park* failed to get the best picture nomination but did in fact score a perfect three out of three in Oscar wins for, Best Visual Effects, Best Sound Mixing and Best Sound Editing. It is quite obvious that Marilyn Monroe was by no means alone when it came to her Oscar snubs. It most certainly has to do with many factors which contribute to both the nomination process as well as the overall final selection process. When you hear the name Marilyn Monroe or see it in print many images immediately enter your mind. The one characteristic that most likely stands out is her voluptuous and extremely beautiful appearance. Then perhaps you will remember her in one of her famous movie appearances. Marilyn Monroe was most definitely an asset to any studio that was lucky enough to have her on their roster of movie stars. Most if not all of the movies that Marilyn Monroe appeared in before her most untimely passing were major box office successes. From a critical point of view a few of the performances Marilyn gave did in fact get rave reviews, from some of the most acclaimed reviewers of her day. When it came time for the holy grail of the movie awards, the Oscars, Marilyn was always absent from the ballots. Marilyn Monroe was never even nominated for an Oscar, even though on more than one occasion she turned in a performance that was

deserving of at the least a nomination. Marilyn Monroe joined a group of some of the best actors and actresses who never won an Oscar and the majority of these household names were never even nominated. The names of these Hollywood giants who were overlooked reads like a who's who of movie star royalty. Iconic stars like Judy Garland, Tony Curtis, and Errol Flynn.

Then there is all three of greatest horror stars of all time, Bela Lagosi, Boris Karloff and Vincent Price. However there are literally hundreds of others who have either been nominated and lost, and those who have never even been nominated regardless of their iconic status as well as their acting ability. In order to fully grasp how enormous the list is and the familiar names that are on it these are the stars who were never nominated. Of course there is

Marilyn Monroe and Errol Flynn but how about Joseph Cotten, Peter Lorre, Mia Farrow, Kim Novak, Maureen O'Hara, Edward G. Robinson, John Barrymore, and Alan Ladd. Certainly every actor and actress might not warrant a nomination but the previous list had some really great performances attached to the names. Continuing with the ones who were never nominated, here is Zero Mostel, Douglas Fairbanks, Sr. and his son Douglas Fairbanks, Jr. The greatest comedian of all time, W.C. Fields, and another iconic comedian Bob Hope, not to mention Jerry Lewis and Buster Keaton. Leading men are on the list, Tyrone Power, Ronald Reagan, Will Rogers, Robert Taylor, Robert Young, Glenn Ford, Martin Sheen, Eli Wallach, and Fred MacMurray. What a list of leading actresses share that dubious distinction, Jean Harlow, Rita Hayworth, Ida Lupino, Shirley Temple, and Tallulah Bankhead. Then there are the actors and actresses who did manage to get nominated but never won. This list has the number of times they were nominated in parenthesis. With the distinction of having the most nominations as an actor, we begin with the actors, Peter O'Toole (8), Richard Burton (7), Arthur Kennedy (5), and

Albert Finney (5). Actresses who were passed over but nominated are, Deborah Kerr (6), Glenn Close (6), Thelma Ritter (6), Irene Dunn (5) and Greta Garbo (4). There are many, many more famous celebrities who managed to make you laugh, brought tears to your eyes and most definitely swept you away to distant places in both your hearts and minds, but as far as Hollywood was concerned their performances were not deserving of an Oscar. The list goes on with, some of your favorite stars, Fred Astaire (1), Charles Bickford (3), Maurice Chevalier (2), Montgomery Clift (4), Kirk Douglas (3), Lillian Gish (1), Cary Grant (2), Angela Lansbury (3), Piper Laurie (3), James Mason (3), Agnes Moorehead (4), Gena Rowlands (2), Rosalind Russell (4), Peter Sellers (2), Barbara Stanwyck (4), Orson Welles (1), Richard Widmark

(1) and John Cassavetes (1). Some of these famous actors and actresses also were sadly overlooked, Lee J. Cobb (2), Raymond Massey (1), Marcello Mastroianni (3), Steve McQueen (1), Adolphe Menjou (1), Burgess Meredith (2), Robert Mitchum (1), Robert Montgomery (2), Tony Curtis (1), Tom Cruise (3), James Dean (2), Clint Eastwood (1), John Garfield (2), Walter Pidgeon (2), William Powell (3), Claude Rains (4), Basil Rathbone (2), Robert Shaw (1), Max Von Sydow (2), Clifton Webb (3), and James Whitmore (2). There are even more famous actresses and here they are, Jane Alexander (4), Judith Anderson (1), Lauren Bacall (1), Marlene Dietrich (1), Ava Gardner (1), Judy Garland (2), Elsa Lanchester (2), Janet Leigh (1), Marsha Mason (4), Merle Oberon (1), Eleanor Parker (3), Michelle Pfeiffer (3), Debbie Reynolds (1), Gene Simmons (2), Kim Stanley (2), Gloria Swanson (3), Gene Tierney (1), Lana Turner (1), Liv Ullmann (2), Tuesday Weld (1), Natalie Wood (3), and Deborah Winger (3). These great actors and actresses brought to life countless characters that will be forever etched in every movie-

goers memory. There will never be another Kane, and there will never be another movie like *Citizen Kane* or *Spartacus*, with a convincing Kirk Douglas in the title role. You will always see Dorothy, a young Judy Garland in the *Wizard of Oz*, following the yellow brick road and proclaiming so vividly, "there's no place like home". How many times have you witnessed Robert Shaw as Quint being devoured by a giant shark in *Jaws*. He played Blondie in *The Good, The Bad and The Ugly* or Marshall Jed Cooper in *Hang 'em High*, as well as Inspector Harry Callahan, in *Dirty Harry* but Clint Eastwood found out repeatedly, apparently these roles were not good enough. *Dracula*, an iconic portrayal by Bela Lagosi, *Frankenstein*, and *The Mummy*, both brought to life by Boris Karloff. The many roles of the stoic Vincent Price, such a Professor Henry Jarrod, in *The House of Wax*, Francois Delambre, in *The Fly* and *The Return of the Fly*, Roderick Usher, in *The House of Usher*, Nicholas Medina in The *Pit and the Pendulum*, and Frederick Loren in *The House on Haunted Hill*, still haunt your memory. For sheer drama how about the character Cal Trask, in *East of Eden* or Jim Stark, *Rebel Without a Cause* or Jett Rink, in *Giant*. These were this actors only movie characters but each and every one was more than memorable, still no Oscar came his way, he was James Dean. There were the eerie gangsters such as Tommy Udo a creepy character Richard Widmark created who sent chills up your spine in *Kiss of Death*, how about the characters Rico in *Little Caesar* and Johnny Rocco, in *Key Largo* brought to life with right on realism, only Edward G. Robinson could bring. This actor's career spanned six decades, but everyone remembers him as the fight promoter Mickey Goodmill in *Rocky*, the raspy cantankerous Burgess Meredith failed to snatch Oscar. Even though he was the definitive Sherlock Holmes, the South African born Basil Rathbone almost got the Oscar in two dramas as Tybalt in *Romeo and Juliet* and King Louis XI, in *If I were King*, almost. This actress was one of Hollywood's brightest and beautiful stars but Ava Gardner couldn't bring home an Oscar as Honey Bear Kelly in *Mogambo*. Three unforgettable roles, first opposite James Dean as Judy, in *Rebel Without a Cause*, then the girl Warren Beatty loved as "Deanie" Loomis, in *Splendor in the Grass*, finally as Angie Rossini Steve Mcqueen's love interest in *Love with the Proper Stranger* left Natalie Wood without the gold. When you get nominated for an Oscar four times and lose four times you wonder what you have to do to win an Oscar. Such was the case of Claude Rains who played his roles to the hilt, first loss was as Senator Joseph Harrison Paine in the great motion picture, *Mr. Smith goes to Washington*. He followed that performance with a role in *Casablanca* as Captain Louis Renault. Only two years later Rains was nominated again playing Job Skeffington in *Mr. Skeffington*, then finally in *Notorious* the Alfred Hitchcock thriller as Alex Sabastian. However two other actors lead the pack in being overlooked when it came to winning an oscar for their numerous nominated roles, a total of fifteen nominations between them. We start with Peter O'Toole, eight nominations spanning over four decades. His first nomination was for *Lawrence of Arabia* in 1962, and his last was for *Venus* in 2006. In between those two movies Peter was nominated for his roles in, Becket, *The Lion in Winter, Goodbye, Mr. Chips, The Ruling Class, The Stunt Man* and *My Favorite Year*. Then there is Richard Burton who had seven nominations starting off with *My Cousin Rachel*, followed by *The Robe* where he brought to the big screen Marcellus Gallio, then the title character in *Becket*. Two years in a row he was passed over for his performances in *The Spy Who Came in from the Cold*, and *Who's Afraid of Virginia Wolfe*. He turned in a memorable performance as King Henry VIII, in *Anne of a Thousand Days*. His last nomination was for his role as a psychiatrist in *Equus*. Actors are not the only ones who have been nominated several times and passed over, many actresses also share that dubious honor. Marsha Mason for example has been nominated four times, first as Maggie Paul in *Cinderella Liberty*, then as Paula McFadden in the *Goodbye Girl*. When she accepted the role of Jennie MacLaine in the hit movie *Chapter Two*, Marsha felt this role would get her an Oscar, it didn't. In the movie, *Only When I Laugh* Marsha played, Georgia, and was nominated a fourth and final time. Another great actress Eleanor Parker was nominated for an Oscar three times. She was extremely versatile and talented, her first nomination was playing the prison inmate, Marie Allen in *Caged*. The very next year she played Kirt Douglas wife, Mary McLeod in *Detective Story*.

Then her portrayal as the opera star Majorie Lawrence in the Oscar winning *Interrupted Melody*. Another great actress who was unable to win an Oscar but was nominated on three occasions was Jane Alexander. In the unforgettable drama *All The Presidents Men*, Jane was nominated for the role as the bookkeeper, Judy Hoback. Two more award winning dramas were able to get Jane noticed and nominated again, *Kramer vs. Kramer* and *Testament*. A pair of extremely gifted actors, one female and the other male each were nominated four times without winning. First, we have Agnes Moorehead who everyone remembers from her T.V. character, Endora in Bewitched but she was first nominated for her role in *The Magnificent Ambersons*. She proved it was no fluke when two years later her name was again on the ballot for her role in *Mrs. Parkington*. Once again a few years later in *Johnny Belinda*, Agnes was nominated and finally over fifteen years later she wowed the critics in *Hush... Hush, Sweet Charlotte*. Her counterpart of sorts was a special actor by the name of Montgomery Cliff. His career was less than twenty years but in his second movie role he managed to get nominated for best actor the movie was *The Search*, and Montgomery actually re-wrote the script. He was a unique actor who when playing a role went the distance such is evident when he was nominated for best actor a second time. For his portrayal of George Eastman in *A Place in the Sun*, Montgomery actually spent a night in jail, confirmation of his desire to perfect his acting skills. Everyone remembers Montgomery for his role in the great war movie, *From Here to Eternity* but he also was nominated in *Judgement at Nuremberg*. Some actresses were prolific in their quest for the Oscar and three were nominated a half of dozen times each. We start with Thelma Ritter who was never really a household name but in a twelve year span was nominated six times, remarkably getting a nomination a record four years in a row. Thelma was nominated in 1950 for her role in *All About Eve*, then in 1951 for wowing audiences in *The Mating Season*. The following year she was again a front runner for the Oscar playing the wise cracking nurse, Clancy in the movie, *With a Song in my Heart*. In 1954 once again Thelma was in top form playing a unique role as Moe, a street peddler in *Pickup on South Street*, most if not all critics agreed she stole the show and was by far going to win an Oscar. She still had something special in the movie *Pillow Talk*, and was nominated once again and finally she played Elizabeth Stroud, the mother of the infamous Robert Stroud, in *Birdman of Alcatraz*. Six unique and powerful roles, six nominations for the coveted Oscar but like so many great actors and actresses, Thelma Ritter was sadly passed over. Next on the list is Deborah Kerr, a distinguished actress who also was nominated six times and some of the movies she was nominated in are true Hollywood Classics. Movies such as the iconic war film, *From Here to Eternity*, where everyone remembers her beach scene with Burt Lancaster, one of Hollywood's greatest kisses. Deborah held her own as a co-star in *The King and I*, opposite Yul Brynner, as well as playing a nun opposite Robert Mitchum in *Heaven Knows Mr. Allison*, two roles that were easily nominated. The other three nominations Deborah received were first for her role opposite Spencer Tracy as his wife in *Edward, My Son*, most critics agree her finest performance. Then in *Separate Tables* opposite David Niven who won the Oscar in that movie, and finally one more nomination for her role in *The Sundowners*, again opposite Robert Mitchum. The last actress to receive six nominations for the Oscar without winning is Glenn Close. For three straight years Glenn was nominated for her performances in *The World According to Garp*, 1982, then the following year in *The Big Chill* and for her role in the 1984 blockbuster, *The Natural*. Her next three nominations were for completely different roles first as a homicidal maniac in *Fatal Attraction*, then in *Dangerous Liaisons* as as a 17th century seductress, and finally in a unique role as a man in *Albert Nobbs*. Two great male actors also have the distinction of being nominated multiple times, five each to be exact and never brought home the gold. The first is Arthur Kennedy, who received his very first nomination for his role in *Champion* playing Kirk Douglas brother. Then only two years later he was nominated again for his role in *Bright Victory* a 1951 war drama. Later in the decade of the 50's Arthur was nominated three more times, in 1955 for *Trial*, in 1957 for *Peyton Place* and finally in 1958 for *Some Came Running*. Five was an unlucky number for Albert Finney who also failed to win an Oscar even though he also was nominated on five separate occasions. Albert truly brought to life the character of *Tom Jones* in the movie of the same name, then a more different role as Inspector Hercule Poirot in *Murder on the Orient Express*. His versatility came to light again in the movie *The Dresser*, for his third nomination. Over twenty years after *Tom Jones*, Albert was nominated for his unique role in *Under the Volcano*. Then finally but hopefully not Albert Finney's last nomination came fifteen years later in *Erin Brockovich*. Clifton Webb began his acting career in 1917 but some twenty seven years later he wowed the critics and audiences with his nominated role in *Laura*. He proved his performance was no fluke as he was nominated two times in the next four years for his once again outstanding performances in *The Razor's Edge* and then *Sitting Pretty*. When a movie fan hears the name Ingmar Bergman the first thing that comes to mind is genius. This next actor made eleven films with Mr. Bergman before receiving his first of two nominations for his 1987 role in *Pelle the Conqueror*. Then almost twenty five years later he was nominated more recently in the unique movie *Extremely Loud and Incredibly Close*, his name is Max von Sydow, and in 2013 he also had another chance starring in *The Letters*. This next actor had a career in motion pictures that spanned over five decades and starred in some of Hollywood's greatest films. His name is James Mason and in 1955 he was nominated for his unique role in the hit *A Star is Born*. Over twenty five years later in 1983 he was nominated for his right on performance in *The Verdict* but failed to win the Oscar. Sandwiched in between those two nominations in 1967 James was nominated for his role in *Georgy Girl*, three great performances that failed to get James Mason an Oscar that he truly deserved. When the name Inspector Jacques Clouseau is mentioned a smile most likely comes to your face. *The Pink Panther* movies were some of the funniest productions that were ever made and all hold up today. Peter Sellers brought to life that iconic character but even though he is best remembered for being a comedic genius, Peter was nominated for two Oscars. The first was in the hit *Dr. Strangelove*, and the second was for his role in *Being There*, both failed to win him the gold. Then we have the great Roman action adventure movie with a cast of Hollywood's biggest male and female stars but one in the title role of *Spartacus* clearly took

over the production. Kirk Douglas was never nominated for his role as *Spartacus* but did manage to get three Academy Award nominations even though he actually should have been nominated a dozen more times. Kirk was nominated in the following movies, *Champion*, *The Bad & The Beautiful* and as a spot on interpretation of Vincent Van Gogh in *Lust For Life*. Whenever a movie buff thinks of Sophia Loren, the name of her male counterpart, Marcello Mastroianni comes to mind. The pair of Italian actors co-starred in fourteen movies in a span of over twenty years. Marcello had a magical style of acting that was so unassuming and that quality was apparent as he was nominated for an Oscar on three occasions. The first nomination was for his role in *Divorce Italian Style*, then for *A Special Day* opposite Sophia Loren and finally for the movie *Dark Eyes*. All three performances were equal in the fact that they all should have brought Marcello an Oscar. In the 1940's and 1950's John Garfield was one of Hollywood's brightest stars. He sadly passed away before the age of forty but managed to get two nominations for an Academy Award. His very first role in 1938 in the movie *Four Daughters* got John a nomination, then several years later he was nominated one last time for his great performance in *Body and Soul.* When you remember how great the movie *On The Waterfront* was, Marlon Brando's Academy Award winning performance comes to mind. Also a standout and nominated for an Academy Award but did not win was Lee J. Cobb. He was an actor of great range and Lee J. Cobb also received a nomination for an Oscar in another Hollywood classic movie, *The Brothers Karamazov.* In just a six year span in the 1940's Charles Bickford was nominated for three Academy Awards but never won. The movies that he wowed the audiences and critics alike were, *The Song of Bernadette, The Farmer's Daughter* and *Johnny Belinda.* It was in that great movie, Johnny Belinda that a great actress Agnes Moorehead was also nominated for her performance but she too lost. Agnes Moorehead was nominated three more times in the movies, *The Magnificent Ambersons, Mrs. Parkington* and in the horror movie, *Hush....Hush, Sweet Charlotte.* Another trio of great actresses who were all nominated on three separate occasions but never were fortunate to win had the distinction of each having a unique style. Angela Lansbury was nominated way back in 1944 for her performance in *Gaslight*, the following year another nomination for *The Picture of Dorian Gray* and finally in 1962 for the *The Manchurian Candidate.* This next actress had great success in the decade of the 1950's with her three nominations, *Caged*, in 1951 followed by *Detective Story* in 1952, then in 1955 for *Interrrupted Melody*, her name was the beautiful Elenor Parker. A span of almost twenty five years between this actresses nominations proved Piper Laurie had that magic to impress audiences for many years. Piper was nominated for her great role in *The Hustler*, 1962, then for *Carrie* in 1976 and finally for *Children of a Lessor God* in 1986. This next actress Rosalind Russell is best remembered for her Oscar nominated performance in *Auntie Mame*, but she was nominated for her dynamic performances three other times. The first was in 1942 in the movie *My Sister Eileen*, then in 1946 for her role in *Sister Kenny*, finally in 1947 for *Mourning Becomes Electra.* "I am big, its the pictures that got small." Just some of the famous words spoken by the character, Norman Desmond, in the movie *Sunset Boulevard*. Gloria Swanson really was the character Norma Desmond in that iconic movie and was nominated for the Oscar. In the late 1920's Gloria Swanson was nominated on two more occasions for her roles in the movies, *Sadie Thompson* and *The Trespasser*. This great dramatic actress was passed over on four separate occasions and failed to win an Oscar. In a span of only eleven years from 1938 to 1949 her unique acting style and screen presence got her roles nominated in the movies, *Stella Dallas, Ball of Fire, Double Indemnity* and *Sorry Wrong Number*. Irene Dunne was mama in the greatest family movie ever made, *I Remember Mama*, and she did get the nomination but not the win. Irene was a seasoned actress long before that performance and she was nominated no less than four more times for her roles in the movies, *Cimarron, Theodora Goes Wild, The Awful Truth* and *Love Affair*. When you are nominated for an Oscar it is a great achievement, when you are nominated numerous times it is an indication you have something special but how about being nominated for two of your roles in the same year. In 1930 Greta Garbo was nominated for an Oscar for two movies, *Anna Christie* and *Romance*. Then on two more occasions she was nominated in 1938 for her role in *Camille*, and in 1940 for *Ninotchka*. Two modern day actresses have each been nominated on three separate occasions. The first is Debra Winger who proved how good she was in the 1983 hit, *An Officer and a Gentleman*, the very next year nominated again for *Terms of Endearment*. A decade later in 1994 Debra Winger was nominated for her great performance in *Shadowlands*. Michelle Pfeiffer had her three Oscar nominations in just five years, first in 1989 for *Dangerous Liaisons*, followed by the 1990 hit, *The Fabulous Baker Boys*, and finally in 1993 for *Love Field*.

It is quite evident that if we evaluate the performances of the iconic Marilyn Monroe she was most definitely not alone when she was clearly overlooked in obtaining an Oscar nomination.

CHAPTER 7

These Performances Should Have Been Noticed

"Keep smiling, because life is a beautiful thing
and there's so much to smile about."

THE YEAR WAS 1955 and Marilyn Monroe had just completed what would be her most controversial movie role to date. There is a very unusual connection between Marilyn and one of Universal Studios greatest horror classic monsters. It was just a year before that *The Creature From the Black Lagoon* was the Universal's biggest horror 3-D box office sensation. Marilyn's movie was *The Seven Year Itch*, a romantic comedy. Right in the middle of the movie, there she is leaving a movie theater that had *The Creature From the Black Lagoon* in big letters on the marque but also had a gigantic statue of the creature on top of the marque as Marilyn and her co-star exited the theater. As they walked down the street Marilyn stated, "I feel sorry for the

Outtake from *The Seven Year Itch* (1952)

creature, he was kinda scary, but all he wanted and needed was some affection, to be loved." Little did Marilyn know when she uttered those words that in the future they would be used to describe her. Moments later as the scene continues, Marilyn stands over a subway grate to experience the breeze. It was a hot summer night and she created one of Hollywood's most iconic scenes in her pleated white halter dress. Here we have two lasting Hollywood icons, one Marilyn Monroe, the epitome of beauty, and the other a horror icon that is one of the top five monsters of all time. *The Seven Year Itch* was a lot better than anyone expected. Most critics felt when they learned it had Marilyn as its star, the movie would be just another vehicle for Marilyn to bring home big box office receipts. However, the critics and the public were very wrong. It had a simple premise, but the way Marilyn handled her role is one of the best ever to grace the screen in terms of romantic comedy. Her delivery coupled with both innocence and seductiveness is virtually unmatched.

Richard Sherman, the male lead played by Tom Ewell is a nerdy, faithful, middle-aged publishing executive with an overactive imagination and a mid-life crisis. His wife Helen, played by Evelyn Keyes, and son Ricky, played by Butch Bernard have left New York City to vacation during the entire summer in Maine. Most of the movie takes place in a small brownstone apartment where Ewell bumps into Marilyn when he returns home after saying goodbye to his family. Now he has the entire summer for himself. The brownstone was on 61st street in Manhattan. Marilyn has just rented the apartment upstairs from him and we find out she is both a commercial actress and former model. Later that evening, Ewell is working on proof reading a book dealing with the subject that a significant proportion of men have extra-marital affairs during the seventh year of marriage. The movie is filled with imaginary sequences that add to the development of how Ewell falls head over heels for Marilyn. A tomato plant tipped over by Marilyn crashes into his lounge chair and when Marilyn apologizes for accidentally knocking it over, Ewell invites her down for a drink. Marilyn pulls no punches and she tells him she has to get dressed and relates how she keeps her underwear cool in her icebox. When she finally makes her way to his apartment, Marilyn was almost too beautiful and glowed as a vision in pink. While they have a drink he lies to her about being married. During this part of the movie Marilyn is portrayed as an innocent young girl, but her sexuality and voluptuous nature was in stark contrast. The pink dress was the perfect color that fit her persona in this particular scene. Marilyn was able to play Ewell like a violin with her role, all the while as he was getting hotter and hotter under the collar. The way she moved around his apartment, the way she sipped from the glass, the way she pouted her lip the way she delivered her lines with a sultry slur all were uniquely Marilyn. This scene is unparalleled by any of her other performances. That is the measurement of a role, of a performance, it is the totality of the way the actress was able to move the audience into emersing themselves in the characterization. Marilyn sees his wedding ring, and he tries to explain the ring but is unconvincing. Marilyn is aloof, she has little or no interest in Ewell. All she wants is his air-conditioning. The scene switches to another one of his fantasy moments and she is now overcome with passion as he plays, Rachmaninoff's Second Piano Concerto, but when the scene reverts back to reality they both innocently play Chopsticks, and without trying Marilyn melts the audience. In a very awkward moment Ewell becomes completely overcome by his fantasies, and he grabs at Marilyn which causes them to fall off the piano bench. Ewell is taken back and he apologizes for his indiscretion but she says it happens to her all the time. It was here that we get more of that Marilyn Monroe charm as he asks her to leave, which she does without making him feel like anything ever happened. In the next few days he becomes more and more drawn to everything that is Marilyn and feels they are getting closer, but in her own subtle way Marilyn just goes about her business Tom Ewell's performance was the perfect compliment for Marilyn Monroe's. Her performance was overlooked for a nomination because she pulled off being the dumb blonde with such artistic perfection it might have been too believable. Does Marilyn Monroe's performance deserve an Oscar nomination? This is another Marilyn Monroe movie that really showcased how special and wonderful Marilyn really was. There will never be a sultry actress that was more adorable or charming. She had many memorable lines

in The Seven Year Itch, such as "I like married men, because you know they're never going to ask you to marry them". Marilyn utters just three little words as Ewell asks her if she wants a cold drink, "that sounds cool!" When this great

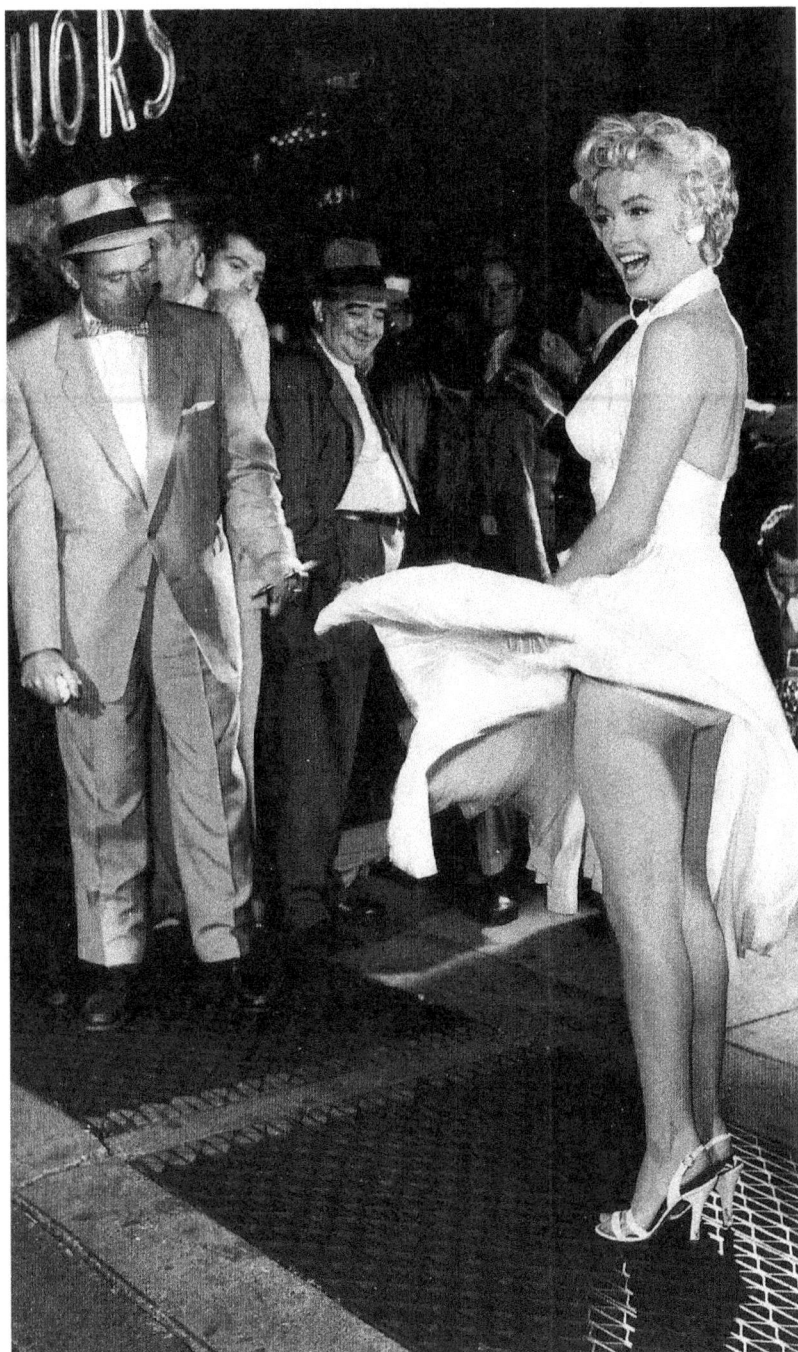

classic movie was made there were many actresses, who attempted to copy that "it" factor that Marilyn had. Even today it can also be said that many have tried to duplicate her but no one ever came close. Now is the right time

to re-visit, The Seven Year Itch, to once again marvel at the childlike aura of this star, to laugh and wonder if Marilyn would have not died at such a young age would she have become the greatest actress of all time. This movie is the first in my list of Marilyn Monroe movies that deserve an Oscar nomination, and is the first leg of Marilyn Monroe's, quest for an Oscar.

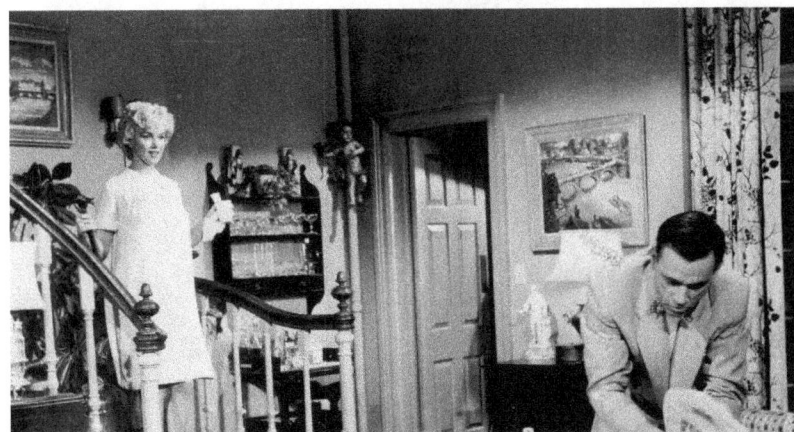

Robert Strauss and Tom Ewell with Marilyn in a rare photo
from *The Seven Year Itch* (1952)

The following year after the success of *The Seven Year Itch*, 20th Century Fox, released *Bus Stop*. It was a big change from Marilyn's, musical and comedic roles. This time Marilyn had a full-fledged dramatic challenge and she met it head on. Her co-stars were all seasoned veterans, Don Murray, Arthur O'Connell, Betty Field, Eileen Heckart, Robery Bray and

Bus Stop (1956)

With Don Murray in *Bus Stop* (1956)

Hope Lange. The movie was a major hit and received numerous award nominations, most notably an Oscar nomination for best supporting actor, Don Murray. The critics were more than kind with their reviews of the movie and the performance of Marilyn Monroe. Most felt it was her breakthrough performance in a movie role as a serious dramatic actress. Marilyn proved she could play any part both of the dumb blonde and her new role as a hardened, Southern chanteuse in search of true love. She managed to convey a whole range of emotions, which were cultivated during her time spent at Lee Strasberg's Actor's Studio in New York. Marilyn was still a very vivacious creature on the big screen and she steals all the scenes she is in. But there is a depth and sympathy to her portrayal of the role that makes you take note of both the performance and also her sheer beauty. To add some confirmation to that observation the director, Joshua Logan according to scriptwriter George Axelrod, stated she would repeatedly break out in tears, become extremely frustrated, forget her lines, and director Joshua Logan couldn't call "cut" during her scenes or she'd take it as a personal affront. Mr. Logan would let literally 100's of feet of film just run out while he calmed her down. Even with these setbacks the chemistry between Marilyn and Don Murray, Marilyn and Arthur O'Connell are outstanding. She was bringing the total

With Arthur O'Connell and Don Murray in *Bus Stop* (1956)

character to life right before your eyes. The character of Cherie, a hillbilly girl who almost married her own cousin when she was only 14 years old. Cherie, was from the Ozarks, a nightclub chanteuse with aspirations of becoming an actress in Hollywood. She immediately captures the heart of a Montana rodeo champion, Bo, played by Don Murray. Bo is quite a character in his own right. He kidnaps Cherie and bundles her off to the roadside bus stop. Gradually, the headstrong Bo learns that you can't rope a gal the same way

With Don Murray in *Bus Stop* (1956)

you lasso a steer, but before this happens there are fights between Bo and other cafe patrons. These fights are related to how all the men in the cafe were mesmerized by Cherie. By this time, Cherie has fallen in love with her impulsive but basically good-hearted abductor. This was a dramatic role for Marilyn, but there is a scene at the cafe, the bus stop where she sings

"That Old Black Magic" the only musical number in the entire production. During the scene she steals the show and it was the moment that the director, Joshua Logan, knew he was getting much more than he expected from his star. Logan was a big supporter of the Lee Strasberg "method" style of acting and he also respected and admired Monroe as an actress. That was the main reason why, before the movie was cast, he went after Marilyn and when it was completed he actually campaigned for her to receive an Oscar nomination. He was very disappointed when the nominations omitted his star. This impeccable Hollywood director was faced with many obstacles during the making of Bus Stop, namely because of the actions of Marilyn Monroe. He cast those differences aside and in the end he felt Marilyn's performance was worthy of an Oscar nomination. Marilyn's great performance was not entirely overlooked, because she did get nominated for a Golden Globe, for her role as Cherie but unfortunately lost. The movie also received a Golden Globe nomination for best motion picture. The other qualities that Marilyn was able to convey were so moving and poignant, there is no doubt you will be emotionally involved. You will be moved to tears on more than one occasion while watching the movie. Marilyn's personal problems paralleled that of her character, it makes you think she wasn't acting at all.

After Marilyn proved herself as a great dramatic actress in *Bus Stop*, she made only one movie under her own production company, Marilyn Monroe Productions. The movie was *The Prince and the Showgirl*, and starred Laurence Olivier, it was produced at Pinewood Studios in England. That movie also had one of Marilyn's unique performances that was greatly overlooked. Her co-star, Laurence Olivier at the time the movie was being made, was regarded as one of Britain's greatest heavyweight actors of the twentieth century. That distinction holds true to today not only for Laurence's work in the movies but also for the classical Shakespearean dramas in which he made his name. Marilyn Monroe was regarded as a lightweight Hollywood starlet who most critics felt was merely utilized for her beauty in a series of undemanding parts. Not so fast, because when the two were on the screen in various scenes the

result was more than evident in that Marilyn actually won those rounds so to speak by a knockout. Each and every time the two heavyweights duked it out Marilyn's mere presence overshadowed the great Olivier who seemed to be overacting. Marilyn was so natural it appeared as if Marilyn really wasn't acting at all, just being Marilyn. It can be noted that there was a strained relationship between Olivier and Monroe during the making of the film. Mr. Olivier had a predetermined opinion about just how good or bad an actress his co-star was. Olivier should have not listened to the critics and on the other hand given Marilyn a fair chance and made his own evaluations of her ability to act. This is really one of Marilyn's best films, there is a unique way she handled her portrayal of Elsie, who comes across as a typical Marilyn type character, very beautiful but excuse the expression, a dumb blonde, but a very likable one. If the film has a weak point it has to be the character of Olivier's, a Grand Duke who really never was convincing. Marilyn was already in her thirties when the film was made, but the naïve and innocent Elsie seems much younger, whereas the middle-aged Charles seems a man old before his time, an impression created as much by his stiffness of manner and bearing as by his grey hair. The gap in the ages of Charles and Elsie seems considerably greater than the nineteen-year gap in the ages of the actors. Whenever they are on screen, it is always Marilyn that one's eyes are drawn to and she gives such a natural performance throughout it almost seems as if she isn't acting at all. She also copes with some extremely tricky dialogue, giving the lie to her inability to remember lines. These are often done in a single take. One scene in particular, early in the film as she is leaving the house before Olivier arrives home, Marilyn is talking rapidly to Richard Wattis as they walk down the long staircase, is outstanding. Marilyn's portrayal of Elsie, a showgirl in England, who has a chance encounter meeting with a visiting Duke (Olivier), from the fictional country of Carpatha (obviously based on Carpathia, Romania). By surprise, Elsie is invited to what turns out to be a private dinner at the embassy residence of the visiting Duke and unexpectedly falls in love with him. Elsie overhears some top secret information and becomes a temporary political pawn between the Duke and his son, about to become king. That is the gist of a rather mundane plot. Marilyn handled her role as the true professional she had become, so this film is quite important in evaluating Marilyn for Oscar consideration. In reality one of the greatest, if not the greatest male actors of all time was upstaged by Marilyn. It had little to do with outward appearances and age differences but everything to do with their performances. Jack Cardiff, the cinematographer, filled the screen with glowing color to match the decor and costumes of the period. That color added to the overall glow of Marilyn. Olivier was also the producer and director. His on screen persona was entertaining but Marilyn truly stole most if not all of the scenes they had together. Once again her method acting experience was paying off. One of the actresses, Sybil Thordyke, her co-star who was cast as the Queen Mother, had a lot to say about Marilyn. What she said was all good such as the profound statement that during the shooting Marilyn was the only one on the set who knew how to act on film and be natural. Even the crew often thought she wasn't acting, that is until the rushes started to show how great Marilyn was on set. Colin Clark, the son of art historian Kenneth Clark, and who later helped establish New York Cities

PBS station, Channel 13 added his praise. Mr. Clark said that when the film was done, despite the endless agony everyone had working with her, Marilyn was "a force of nature" onscreen. Both Marilyn and Olivier were nominated for their respective performances as Best Actress and Actor by The British Film Academy. Marilyn was also nominated by both the French Film Academy, and the Italian Film Academy for Best Actress. Marilyn won The Crystal Star Award, The French Film Academy's equivalent to the Oscar. Olivier did a good job portraying his comic character, with an appropriate, but a little over the top German accent, Olivier, was out shined by Marilyn even though her role as Elsie had many limitations. The character was a very weak one but she made the most of it, bringing spontaneity, improvisation, good comic timing, playfulness and charm to the lightweight role. It's one of Monroe's best acting performances, comparable to her Golden Globe Award winning role as Sugar Cane, in the classic Billy Wilder comedy *Some Like It Hot*, 1959.

When you think of the movie, *Some Like it Hot*, most likely you recall an image of Marilyn Monroe. There she is all decked out in one of her unique sexy costumes running down a hotel lobby or cramped in a train sleep away bunk with a bunch of girls. The fact of the matter is the movie also had in the cast two of the most legendary male movie stars, as well as a list of supporting actors and actresses that reads like a who's who of Hollywood greats. The director, Billy Wilder was one of Hollywood's greatest directors of all time, racking up a total of twenty-one Academy Award nominations and winning six Oscars. Mr. Wilder assembled a cast that featured Jack Lemmon and Tony Curtis in leading roles and George Raft, Joe E. Brown, Pat O'Brien and Nehemiah Persoff in supporting ones. This is by far one of the movies that Marilyn literally solidified herself for all time in movie lore by not only playing herself but by mastering all the nuances she learned at Lee Strasberg's school of method acting. There are many reasons why the diversified performance that Marilyn turned in is deserving at the least a nomination for the Oscar. In her very first scene in the movie it was not what she said but how she carried herself on the big screen that made the audience take notice. First, before Marilyn's performance is evaluated for an Oscar nomination,

With Tony Curtis and George Raft

a short look at the movie. It has the distinction of being ranked number one on The American Film Institute's top one hundred comedies. Both Tony Curtis and Jack Lemmon were perfect in their roles but the entire movie was a fast moving production that is entertaining the first time you see it or even after a hundred viewings. It truly is a virtual masterpiece of cinematic genius. There are numerous sub-plots and outstanding supporting characters, never slow or boring. So, how did Marilyn manage to mesmerize the audience in a movie with so many positive elements? It was simple, Marilyn was once again just being Marilyn. Her timeless beauty, her walk her sultry voice, even her beautiful hair all sparkled on the screen. It was another black and white production but you might swear and imagine you were watching Marilyn glowing in color. The one quality that you will take away from the performance Marilyn gave is summed up in two words, soft and sweet. Marilyn's character, Sugar might have been a planned name. I doubt that fact because even the award winning director, Billy Wilder, had no idea Marilyn would create "Sugar" the way she did. Instead of using all her exotic charms to seduce Tony Curtis, Marilyn transforms into one of the softest and sweetest girls you will ever see. She is kind, gentle, sweet, like her namesake. She is beyond loving, Marilyn was magical and her character is one you want to know, want to meet. That interpretation was all coming from inside Marilyn, she was all loving, but soft and gentle at heart. Watch the movie and it is for certain you will agree with this evaluation. You will see what has made Marilyn the most glamorous actress of all time. She was soft and sweet. It may sound repetitive but it will never be duplicated by any woman as voluptuous as Marilyn. She sort of cast aside her erotic appearance and became childlike and vulnerable. When you think of the first time you fell in love, or think about the girl next door or even remember a love that got away. "Sugar" is that girl, you will never erase their memories, never.

The Misfits (1961)

In what would prove to be her very last released movie role, Marilyn Monroe delivered another of her greatest performances. If you have viewed the movie you already know that you will never forget the character that Marilyn brought to life. Perhaps it was really Marilyn you were watching and not the character Roslyn Tabler, she created. One thing is for sure, you will never

forget them both. Arthur Miller one of America's greatest playwrites' most likely created the character of Roslyn for his wife, Marilyn. The movie was *The Misfits* and featured two of Hollywood's most dynamic male actors. These actors can be mentioned in the same breath as any of the greatest actors of all time. Clark Gable who was one of Marilyn's co-stars in *The Misfits*, like Marilyn, also died prematurely. Clark passed away less than two weeks after the completion of the movie. The other male lead Montgomery Cliff proved to be the perfect compliment not only to Marilyn's character Roslyn Tabler but in real life as well. In one of the opening scenes Marilyn tells Perce Howland, Montgomery's character, "You're the only person I ever met who's more screwed up then me." Roslyn Tabler was a very complex, adrift, loving but very conscientious human being. When the movie was released it was not reviewed favorably by the critics, mainly because it was determined years later that this very unique production was actually well ahead of its time. It was a movie that had such deep and profound messages and performances that the untimely demise of both Clark Gable and Marilyn overshadowed its importance and place in cinematic history. The movie and the performance turned in by Marilyn has to be looked at with a precise evaluation because it was Marilyn's last attempt at proving to Hollywood she was so much more

than just a sex symbol, the title that followed her since the very beginning of her short career. First we will look at the movie and how even though it is a forgotten movie of sorts, today it is now coming forward in the lexicon of film history as an underrated gem. The theme was misunderstood for many reasons. When it was released, the decade of the 1960's was filled with much controversy, and changes. The three male characters, Gay, Guido and Perce are a bunch of washed up individuals. Soon after the tone of the movie is set and the various introductions of all the main players we have a unique situation evolve. The three men prepare to go after wild mustangs and sell them for of all things dog food. Roslyn reluctantly goes along with the men and in a memorable scene the men catch a stallion and four mares, Roslyn becomes enraged and she screams that she hates the men when she learns that the mustangs will be sold for dog food. It is in this scene that Marilyn's complete range of emotions light up the screen. Of course she is her usual caldron of molton sexuality, without trying, this time in jeans. Her rage at the mere thought of those beautiful horses being tied and slaughtered will reach your innermost emotions. Arthur Miller's screenplay complements the unusual theme and is no doubt one of his most striking works. It paints a magnificent but somewhat morbid story of a group of lost souls, individuals all lost in the wide expanse of the West in search of the discarded essence of their misspent lives. The film's beautiful cinematography by Russell Metty stands out as superb artistry at the demise of the black and white era of motion pictures. It is highlighted beautifully with the silver of the deep expanse of the desert and the flat grays and blacks of the distant mountains upon which the last act of the movie is shot. Much like the soundtracks of the great Erich Wolfgang Korngold, the music of Alex North is among his best work and gives a unique touch to the aerial scenes and the round up at the end of the wild mustangs. Alex North created a mood during the entire production. The music captured the audience, right from the opening credits. Montgomery Clift, who was unknowingly at the very last years of his short life was more than believable and touching in his performance of Perce. This broken down cowboy with the broken heart. Montgomery's performance is at times almost too painful to watch. When Perce decides to make a phone call home to his mother you will agree it is one of the cinemas most moving moments between a mother and her lost son. Perce, named after Perecival, one of the knight's of the round table, is seeking the unattainable through sacrificing his body to the Rodeo. It is clear that he won't last much longer. Arthur Miller made sure

this character would move the audience by staying drunk as his way of dealing with the hurt and pain in his life. Another dynamic performance is turned in by the consummate character actor, Eli Wallach. He pulls at your heart with a strong deeply moving portrait of Guido who has lost his wife, his way, and his humanity. When Wallach plays opposite Marilyn in a scene where he asks her to save him, once again it will touch you deeply. The unique moody style of Arthur Miller came through brilliantly as all of the characters, though different, each shared in a multitude of problems. Guido was a pilot who has lost the most, Guido had the most to lose. World War II took him away from medical studies and put him in the cockpit of a heavy bomber. Then his wife died because a flat tire prevented him from getting her to medical attention in time, an excuse that Roslyn astutely recognizes as a weak cop-out that gave him permission to stop trying. He even offers to sell out his friends and spare the horses in the movie if Roslyn will leave Gay for him. Then we have the versatile female character actress Thelma Ritter who brought her character to life in her usual way of short wisecracks. This time her performance as Isabelle is filled with those one liners but each with an underlying sadness and vulnerability. She is the aging divorcée Isabelle Steers who claims that the only real men left in the world are cowboys.

As Gay Langland, Clark Gable gives what just might also be considered as the best performance of his entire career. This will be contemplated as a rather bold statement but if you understand it was a wise choice for Gable to take on the role of Langland. On the surface it looked to be just another one of his typical macho made to fit parts. Soon after the story unfolds it is evident that Arthur Miller's character Gay, reveals that beneath his gruff, not a care in the world, very tough guy persona, there is also a cowboy and a man in deep pain and despair at his many losses. The world has left him behind, he has been abandoned by his children, the ones in his life that mean the most to what he has left. The drunken Gable breaks down so violently, it is a shock to watch this once great man fall apart. He has many memorable quotes and one, sums up the plight of all the characters when he states, "You can't lasso a dream," he says. To his credit, he accepts the inevitability of change instead

of feeling sorry for himself. This shows he has hope and fortitude. Isabelle was right, he is a real man. This is Clark Gable, the actor that brought to the screen so many great memorable performances but perhaps it can be said that this might be his finest ever. In many ways it rivals Mr. Gable's performance in the classic, *Gone With The Wind*, he reached down deep and was able to capture the emotions of Rhett Butler but this time he was complimented by Marilyn Monroe. Three very troubled, very messed up over the hill cowboys. Any one of which would have been enough for any actress to play against with believability. Any one of the three actors' performances could have been nominated for an Oscar in a movie with half of the artistic qualities of this great cinematic masterpiece. Gable, Cliff, and Wallach, the three Misfits each were upstaged by the movie's biggest Misfit, Monroe. It can be stated that you will agree, all the scenes with Marilyn Monroe and any one of the three actors, display how Marilyn's performance was equivalent to theirs. She will

tear at your innermost emotions. She will bring tears to your eyes. You will be thoroughly convinced these are real misfits, they are real people, and not some characters in a movie. Marilyn, as captivating as she was with the three men, could also be captivating with Isabelle Steers, the character created by Thelma Ritter.

The director was John Huston, the Hollywood heavyweight who was nominated for an Oscar fifteen times and won twice. Marilyn Monroe gave an astounding performance as Roslyn Tabler the newly divorced dancer. Roslyn is a very sad troubled woman who finds in the company of the three aforementioned men something to finally live for, she actually finds adventure and hope, as well as gets back to living her life. It is a performance that shows many different emotions that Marilyn possessed right from her very first time on the big screen. This time the emotions were amplified and strongly influenced by her personal downfalls. Both the director John Huston and the screenwriter, Arthur Miller molded a troubled Marilyn in order to create her stunning Roslyn. It was Marilyn, sometimes looking much younger, even teenage like in some scenes that was able to create and maintain Roslyn from start to finish of the movie. There are no bad moments for Marilyn, each and every scene is perfection, you will cry by her performance, not once but on numerous occasions. This, her last performance is her best and the true example of the collaborative creation that the art of film really is. Even though Marilyn was as troubled off the screen as on, she divorced Arthur Miller during production. Marilyn was so good, it is a testament to her talent as an actress and a star. Look closely at her mannerisms when she is listening to the other actors read their parts. This is Marilyn at her best, where she had no equal because along with her acting she brought a true beauty and wholesomeness, this is the true mark of a great screen actor. To be able to listen and draw the audience into the inner life of the character through that deceptively simple act of listening and reaction. This among all of Marilyn's other attributes was her gift to the audience. Her scene with Montgomery Cliff in the back of the bar, sitting on a pile of trash, her scene with Eli Wallach in the speeding car, and on the bridge with Thelma Ritter after her divorce. These are only a few examples in this film of her great talent. In the 1950's and early 60's there were only a handful of great young actresses in film, Elizabeth Taylor, and Marilyn Monroe where at the summit of that very small mountain.

Once again there would be no nomination for Marilyn Monroe, this time and for the very last time for her outstanding performance in *The Misfits*. The other actresses who were nominated that year were, Sophia Loren in *Two Women*, Audrey Hepburn in *Breakfast at Tiffany's*, Geraldine Page in *Summer and Smoke*, Natalie Wood in *Splendor in the Grass* and Piper Laurie in *The Hustler*. Of note, the Oscar went to Sophia Loren. *The Misfits* like Marilyn received no nominations in any category.

CHAPTER 8

Quotes

"You never know what life is like, until you have lived it."
—Marilyn

"Only in the contemplation of beauty is human life worth living."
—Plato

A PERSON'S LIFE IS MEASURED by their achievements and the people that they touched along life's journey. Some individuals live to eighty or ninety years of age and never leave even one prophetic or meaningful quote during all those years. Other individuals are remembered for the quotes they said and in some cases those quotes have become a sort of trademark that we associate with the person. A good example of this statement is the great historian, Will Rogers. Everyone knows and immediately thinks of his quote, "I never met a man I didn't like," at the mere mention of his name. Another unmistakable quote, "Come up and see me some time", is one that makes you envision the

Niagara (1953)

Niagara test shot (1953)

Niagara outtake (1953)

actress, Mae West, one of Hollywood's most controversial stars. Folklore hero, Davy Crockett, uttered, "Be sure you're right then go ahead." Even the unforgettable movie star Bruce Lee is also remembered for his wisdom and philosophy not withstanding entire books of his memorable quotes. Just a few of his deepest ones are very, very profound. Bruce Lee on life: "To know oneself is to study oneself in action with another person." On love: "Love is like a friendship caught on fire. In the beginning a flame, very pretty often hot and fierce, but still only light and flickering. As love grows older, our hearts mature and our love becomes as coals, deep-burning, and unquenchable." On martial arts: "I fear not the man who has practiced 10,000 kicks once, but I fear the man who has practiced one kick 10,000 times." One of Hollywood's most controversial

Publicity photo for *River of No Return* (1954)

male actors Errol Flynn uttered the words, "It's not what they say about you, it's what they whisper." Two quotes that might directly apply to Marilyn Monroe and how she carried herself through her short thirty-six years of life were spoken by great men. Ralph Waldo Emerson said, "To be yourself in a world that is constantly trying to make you something else is the greatest accomplishment." All of Hollywood and the world were trying to do just that to Marilyn, both on and off the screen. Oscar Wilde summed up Marilyn with just one unique sentence, a unique look at one's life. "To live is the rarest thing in the world. Most people exist, that is all." Marilyn made it a habit of

River of No Return (1954)

always speaking her mind. She was not afraid of what people thought of her or how she behaved. The following list of Marilyn's quotes is just a sampling of the many profound statements which are attributed to her. Even though a few of the quotes that follow might not have come directly from Marilyn, the quotes have always been associated as ones made by her. There are many included here that could have been mistaken for some great philosopher, some person who evaluated their surroundings and gave to the world codes to live by. These quotes will show beyond a shadow of a doubt that Marilyn Monroe was so much more, so definitively extraordinary in everything she did. So without any further introductions I give you the quotes, but first:

> "This above all; to thine own self be true, and it must follow,
> as the night the day, Thou canst not then be false to any man."
> —*William Shakespeare.*

With Robert Mitchum in *River of No Return* (1954)

River of No Return (1954)

River of No Return (1954)

With Tommy Rettig in *River of No Return* (1954)

"Marilyn Monroe, in her own words......

"No one ever told me I was pretty when I was a little girl. All little girls should be told they're pretty, even if they aren't."

"Hollywood is a place where they pay you a thousand dollars for a kiss and fifty cents for your soul. I know, because I turned down the first offer often enough and held out for the fifty cents."

"My first contract with 20ᵗʰ Century-Fox was like my first vaccination, it didn't take."

Relaxing on the set of *River of No Return* (1954)

"I learned to walk as a baby and I haven't had a lesson since."

"The way it is the individual is the underdog, and with all the things a corporation has going for them the individual comes out banged on her head. The artist is nothing. It's really tragic."

"Acting isn't something you do. Instead of doing it, it occurs. If you're going to start with logic, you might as well give up. You can have conscious preparation, but you have unconscious results."

"I kept driving past the theater with my name on the marquee. Was I excited. I wished they were using 'Norma Jean' so that the kids at home and schools who never noticed me could see it."

Some Like it Hot (1959)

"An actress is not a machine, but they treat you like a machine. A money machine."

"I am not a victim of emotional conflicts. I am human."

"Only the public can make a star. It's the studios who try to make a system out of it."

"Someone said to me, "If fifty percent of the experts in Hollywood said that you had no talent and should give up, what would you do?" My answer was then and still is, if one hundred percent told me that, all one hundred percent would be wrong."

Some Like it Hot (1959)

"A career is wonderful, but you can't curl up with it on a cold night."

"What do I wear in bed? Why, Chanel No. 5 of course."

"Boys think girls are like books, if the cover doesn't catch their eye, they won't bother to read what's inside."

"The real lover is the man who can thrill you by kissing your forehead or smiling into your eyes or just staring into space."

"I don't mind living in a man's world, as long as I can be a woman in it."

Some Like it Hot (1959)

Some Like it Hot (1959)

"A strong man doesn't have to be dominant toward a woman. He doesn't match his strength against a woman weak with love for him. He matches it against the world."

"I am good, but not an angel. I do sin, but I am not the devil. I am just a small girl in a big world trying to find someone to love."

"If I'd observed all the rules I'd never have got anywhere."

"It takes a smart brunette to play a dumb blond."

"An actor is supposed to be a sensitive instrument. Isaac Stern takes good care of his violin. What if everyone jumped on his violin?"

Some Like it Hot (1959)

"That's the way you feel when you're beaten inside. You don't feel angry at those who've beaten you. You just feel ashamed."

"With fame, you know, you can read about yourself, somebody else's ideas about you, but what's important is how you feel about yourself-for survival and living day to day with what comes up."

"Success makes so many people hate you. I wish it wasn't that way. It would be wonderful to enjoy success without seeing envy in the eyes of those around you."

"I'm not interested in money, I just want to be wonderful."

"I don't stop when I'm tired. I stop when I'm done."

Some Like it Hot (1959)

"Goethe said, "Talent is developed in privacy, you know? And it's really true. There is a need for aloneness which I don't think most people realize for an actor. It's almost having certain kinds of secrets for yourself that you'll let the whole world in on only for a moment, when you're acting."

"My great ambition is to have people comment on my fine dramatic performances."

"Everybody says I can't act. They said the same thing about Elizabeth Taylor. And they were wrong. She was great in A Place in the Sun. I'll never get the right part, anything I really want. My looks are against me. They're too specific."

"When it comes down to it, I let them think what they want. If they care enough to bother with what I do, then I'm already better than them."

As Sugar Kane in Some Like it Hot (1959)

Sugar Kane and Joe (Tony Curtis) in Some Like it Hot (1959)

"I think if other girls know how bad I was when I started they'll
be encouraged. I finally made up my mind I wanted to be an actress-
and I was not going to let my lack of confidence ruin my chances."

"My illusions didn't have anything to do with being a fine actress. I knew
how third rate I was. I could actually feel my lack of talent, as if it were
cheap clothes I was wearing inside. But my God, how I wanted to learn, to
change, to improve."

"If I play a stupid girl and ask a stupid question, I've got to follow it
through. What am I supposed to do, look intelligent?"

"You sit alone. It's night outside. Automobiles roll down Sunset Boulevard
like an endless string of beetles. Their rubber tires make a purring high-
class noise. You're hungry and you say, it's not good for my waistline to eat.
There's nothing finer than a washboard belly."

Sugar Kane and company in Some Like it Hot (1959)

"I used to think as I looked out on the Hollywood night, there must be thousands of girls sitting alone like me, dreaming of becoming a movie star. But I'm not going to worry about them. I'm dreaming the hardest."

"Imperfection is beauty. Madness is genius and it is better to be absolutely ridiculous than absolutely boring."

"You believe lies so you eventually learn to trust no one but yourself."

"For those who are poor in happiness, each time is a first time; happiness never becomes a habit."

"It's better to be absolutely ridiculous than absolutely boring."

Some Like it Hot (1959)

Some Like it Hot (1959)

Let's Make Love (1960)

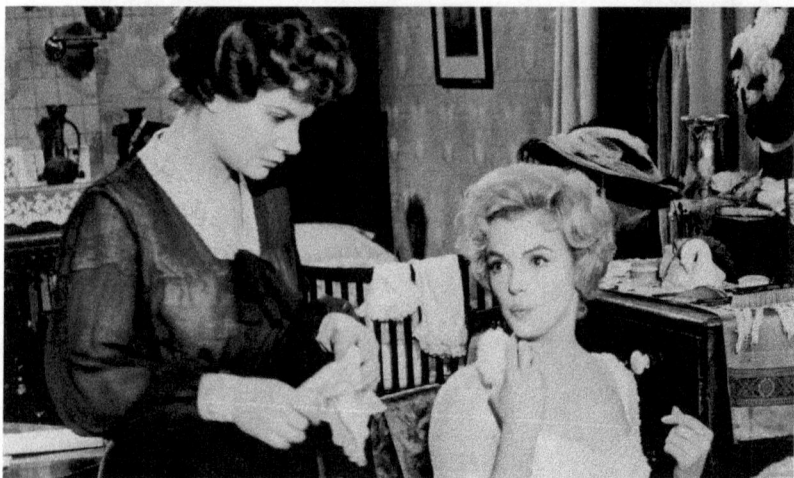

The Prince and the Showgirl (1957)

"Just because you fail once, doesn't mean you fail at everything. Keep trying, hold on, and always trust yourself, because if you don't then who will?"

"Looking back, I guess I used to play-act all the time. For one thing, it meant I could live in a more interesting world than the one around me."

"I read poetry to save time."

"I've often stood silent at a party for hours listening to my movie idols turn into dull and little people."

"I live to succeed, not to please you or anyone else."

The Prince and the Showgirl (1957)

The Prince and the Showgirl (1957)

"I'm definitely a woman and I enjoy it."

"Your clothes should be tight enough to show you're a woman but loose enough to show you're a lady."

"All a girl really wants is for one guy to prove to her that they are not the same."

"I could never pretend something I didn't feel. I could never make love if I didn't love, and if I loved I could no more hide the fact than change the color of my eyes."

"A girl doesn't need anyone who doesn't need her."

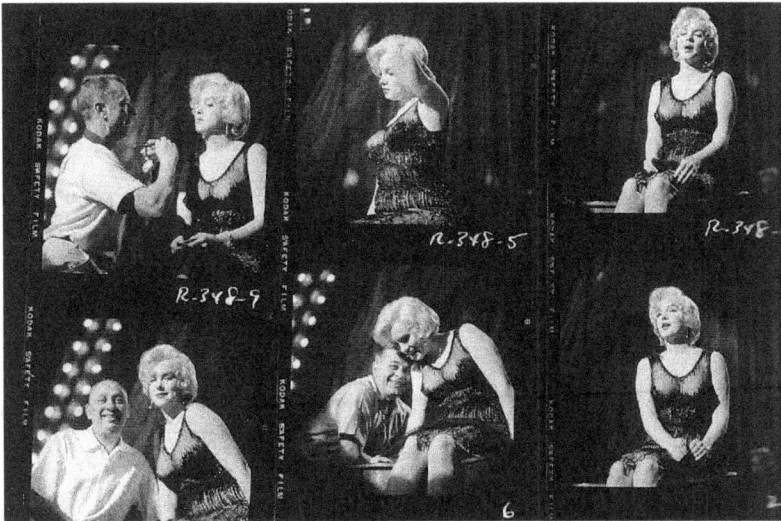

Some Like it Hot (1959)

"I don't forgive people because I'm weak, I forgive them because I am strong enough to know people make mistakes."

"Wanting to be someone else is a waste of the person you are."

"I never intentionally mean to hurt anyone, but you can't be too nice to people you work with, else they will trample you to death."

"There was my name up in lights. I said God, somebody's made a mistake. But there it was, in lights. And I sat there and said, Remember, you're not a star. Yet there it was up in lights."

"I have too many fantasies to be a housewife.....I guess I am a fantasy."

"A sex symbol becomes a thing, I hate being a thing."

"It's better to be unhappy alone than unhappy with someone."

"It's often just enough to be with someone. I don't need to touch them. Not even talk. A feeling passes between you both. You're not alone."

"I restore myself when I'm alone. A career is born in public, talent in privacy."

"I won't be satisfied until people want to hear me sing without looking at me."

"I used to say to myself. What the devil have you got to be proud about, Marilyn Monroe? And I'd answer: Everything, everything, and I'd walk slowly and turn my head slowly as if I were a queen."

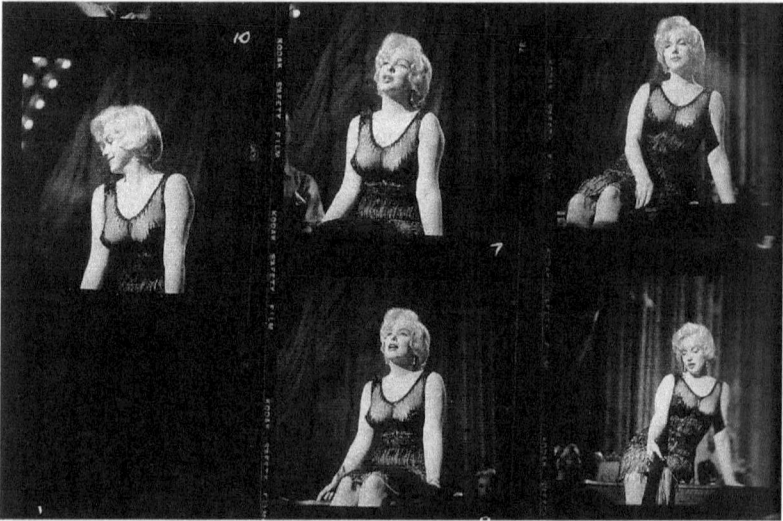

Some Like it Hot (1959)

"Fame will go by and, so long, I've had you, fame. If it goes by, I've always known it was fickle. So at least it's something I experience, but that's not where I live."

"My travels have always been of the same kind. No matter where I've gone or why I've gone there it ends up that I never see anything. Becoming a movie star is living on a merry-go-round. When you travel you take the merry-go-round with you. You don't see natives or new scenery. You see chiefly the same press agents, the same sort of interviewers, and the same picture layouts of yourself."

"I feel as though it's all happening to someone right next to me. I'm close, I can feel it, I can hear it, but it really isn't me."

"The nicest thing for me is sleep, then at least I can dream."

"I want to grow old without facelifts. I want to have the courage to be loyal to the face I have made."

"Dreaming about being an actress, is more exciting than being one."

"Maybe I'll never be able to do what I hope to do, but at least I have hope."

"Fame is like caviar, you know -- it's good to have caviar but not when you have it at every meal".

"The truth is I've never fooled anyone. I've let people fool themselves. They didn't bother to find out who and what I was".

"When you have only a single dream it is more than likely to come true— because you keep working toward it without getting mixed up".

"I'm looking forward to eventually becoming a marvelous-excuse the word marvelous-character actress. Like Marie Dressler, like Will Rogers."

"Every morning I walk across my apartment rolling an empty soda bottle between my ankles, in order to preserve my balance."
"I have never been very good at being a member of any group—more than a group of two, that is."

"Fame is fickle and I know it. It has its compensations, but it also has its drawbacks and I've experienced them both."

"Beneath the makeup and behind the smile I'm just a girl who wishes for the world."

"I don't mind being burdened with being glamorous and sexual. Beauty and femininity are ageless and can't be contrived, and glamour, although the manufacturers won't like this, cannot be manufactured. Not real glamour; it's based on femininity."

"I have feelings too. I am still human. All I want is to be loved, for myself and for my talent."

"I had to use my wits or else I'd have been sunk – and nothing is going to sink me. Everyone was always pulling at me, tugging at me, as if they wanted a piece of me. It was always, 'do this, do that', and not just on the job but off, too. God I've tried to stay intact, whole."

"We should all start to live before we get too old. Fear is stupid. So are regrets."

"I didn't pay much attention to the whistles and whoops, in fact, I didn't quite hear them. I was full of a strange feeling, as if I were two people. One of them was Norma Jeane from the orphanage who belonged to nobody,

the other was someone whose name I didn't know. But I knew where she belonged, she belonged to the ocean and the sky and the whole world."

"She was a girl who knew how to be happy even when she was sad."

"Keep trying, hold on, and always, always, always believe in yourself, because if you don't then who will?"

"They will only care when you're gone."

. . . .

"I'm going to be a great movie star some day."

CHAPTER 9

Filmography

"I restore myself when I'm alone. A career is born in public—
talent in privacy."

All About Eve 1950 - N/R, 138 min.
Genre: Drama
Director: Joseph L. Mankiewicz
Cast: Bette Davis, Anne Baxter, George Sanders, Celeste Holm, Gary Merrill, Thelma Ritter, Marilyn Monroe, Hugh Marlowe, Gregory Ratoff, Barbara Bates, Walter Hampden, Randy Stuart, Craig Hill

This Oscar winner for Best Picture, Director, Supporting Actor (George Sanders), and three other awards tells the story of young actress Eve's (Anne Baxter) attempts to reach stardom without paying her dues by joining a group of famous Broadway types. A candid and humorous look at New York theater is the result. Bette Davis: "Fasten your seatbelts. It's going to be a bumpy ride." The film also received eight other Oscar nominations including two for Best Actress (Bette Davis and Anne Baxter) and two for Supporting Actress (Celeste Holm and Thelma Ritter). The 14 total nominations tied 1997's "Titanic" as the most received by any film.

Cast

Bette Davis	Margo Channing
Anne Baxter	Eve Harrington
George Sanders	Addison DeWitt
Celeste Holm	Karen Richards
Gary Merrill	Bill Sampson
Thelma Ritter	Birdie Coonan
Marilyn Monroe	Miss Caswell
Hugh Marlowe	Lloyd Richards
Gregory Ratoff	Max Fabian
Barbara Bates	Phoebe
Walter Hampden	Master of Ceremonies
Randy Stuart	Girl
Craig Hill	Leading Man

As Young as You Feel 1951 /R, 77 min.
Genre: Comedy
Director: Harmon Jones
Cast: Monty Woolley, Thelma Ritter, David Wayne, Jean Peters, Constance Bennett, Marilyn Monroe, Russ Tamblyn, Roger Moore, Allyn Joslyn, Albert Dekker, Clinton Sundberg, Minor Watson, Wally Brown, Gerald Oliver Smith, Frank Wilcox

John Hodges (Monty Woolley) is faced with forced retirement at age 65. When retirement does not fit into his lifestyle, he sets out to change company

policy by impersonating the president of the parent company and tries to get rid of the age rule for retirement. Of course, complications ensue.

Cast

Monty Woolley	John R. Hodges
Thelma Ritter	Della Hodges
David Wayne	Joe Elliott
Jean Peters	Alice Hodges
Constance Bennett	Lucille McKinley
Marilyn Monroe	Harriet
Russ Tamblyn	Willie McKinley
Roger Moore	Saltenstall
Allyn Joslyn	George Hodges
Albert Dekker	Louis McKinley
Clinton Sundberg	Frank Erickson
Minor Watson	Harold P. Cleveland
Wally Brown	Horace Gallagher
Gerald Oliver Smith	McKinleys' Butler
Frank Wilcox	Joe, Cleveland's Lawyer

The Asphalt Jungle 1950 N/R, 112 min.

Genre: Drama

Director: John Huston

Cast: Sterling Hayden, Louis Calhern, Sam Jaffe, James Whitmore, Marilyn Monroe, Strother Martin, Marc Lawrence, Jean Hagen, John McIntire, Anthony Caruso, Teresa Celli, Barry Kelley, Brad Dexter, John Maxwell, Dorothy Tree

Recently paroled Erwin "Doc" Riedenschneider (Sam Jaffe) gathers together a gang of criminals–Dix Handley (Sterling Hayden), Gus Ninissi (James Whitmore), and Louis Ciavelli (Anthony Caruso)–and attempts to commit

the perfect crime. A corrupt lawyer, Alonzo D. Emmerich (Louis Calhern), backs a jewel robbery, and the safe is blown up and the jewels are robbed, but the scheme is doomed from the start. Academy Award nominations include Best Director and Supporting Actor (Sam Jaffe).

Cast

Sterling Hayden	Dix Handley
Louis Calhern	Alonzo D. Emmerich
Sam Jaffe	Doc Erwin Reidenschneider
James Whitmore	Gus Minissi
Marilyn Monroe	Angela Phinlay
Strother Martin	William Doldy
Marc Lawrence	Cobby
Jean Hagen	Doll Conovan
John McIntire	Police Commissioner Hardy
Anthony Caruso	Louis Ciavelli
Teresa Celli	Maria Ciavelli

Barry Kelley	Lt. Ditrich
Brad Dexter	Bob Brannom
John Maxwell	Dr. Swanson
Dorothy Tree	May Emmerich

Bus Stop 1956 N/R, 96 min.
Genre: Comedy / Drama / Romance
aka: *The Wrong Kind of Girl*

Director: Joshua Logan
Cast: Marilyn Monroe, Don Murray, Arthur O'Connell, Hope Lange, Hans
Conried, Betty Field, Eileen Heckart, Robert Bray, Max Showalter, Henry

Slate, Terry Kelman, Pete Logan, Jack Martin, Edward G. Robinson Jr., Andy Womack

A waitress, Cherie (Marilyn Monroe), dreams of her name in lights in Hollywood. Don Murray plays Bo, a cowboy, who becomes enamored with Cherie and thinks she is the "angel" he wants to marry.

Cast

Marilyn Monroe	Cherie
Don Murray	Beauregard "Bo" Decker
Arthur O'Connell	Virgil Blessing
Hope Lange	Elma Duckworth
Hans Conried	*Life Magazine* Photographer
Betty Field	Grace
Eileen Heckart	Vera
Robert Bray	Carl
Max Showalter	*Life Magazine* Reporter
Henry Slate	Night Club Manager
Terry Kelman	Gerald
Pete Logan	Announcer
Jack Martin	Rodeo Cowboy
Edward G. Robinson Jr.	Cowboy
Andy Womack	Clown

Clash by Night 1952 N/R, 105 min.

Genre: Drama

Director: Fritz Lang

Cast: Barbara Stanwyck, Paul Douglas, Robert Ryan, Marilyn Monroe, J. Carrol Naish, Keith Andes, Silvio Minciotti, Julius Tannen, Mario Siletti

Mae (Barbara Stanwyck) returns to her hometown after an absence of 10 years and marries a fisherman, Jerry (Paul Douglas). She raises a family but cannot seem to stay away from a rough-around-the-edges projectionist (Robert Ryan) who seems to understand her restless unhappiness.

Don't Bother to Knock 1952 N/R, 76 min.
Genre: Drama
Director: Roy Ward Baker
Cast: Richard Widmark, Marilyn Monroe, Anne Bancroft, Donna Corcoran, Jeanne Cagney, Jim Backus, Verna Felton, Lurene Tuttle, Elisha Cook Jr., Willis Bouchey

Nell (Marilyn Monroe) is a psychotic woman who becomes unhinged while hired as a babysitter for guests at a hotel.

The Fireball 1950 N/R, 83 min.
Genre: Drama
Director: Tay Garnett
Cast: Mickey Rooney, Pat O'Brien, Beverly Tyler, James Brown, Marilyn Monroe, Milburn Stone, Ralph Dumke, Sam Flint, Glenn Corbett, Bert Begley, John Hedloe, James Anderson, Al Hill, Kenner G. Kemp, Frank Mills

Johnny Cesar (Mickey Rooney) lived in a Catholic orphanage, headed by Father O'Hara (Pat O'Brien), until he ran away. Now, he is a roller derby star but is stricken with polio and is about to learn even more about life.

Cast

Mickey Rooney	Johnny Casar
Pat O'Brien	Father O'Hara
Beverly Tyler	Mary Reeves

James Brown	Allen
Marilyn Monroe	Polly
Milburn Stone	Jeff Davis
Ralph Dumke	Bruno Crystal
Sam Flint	Dr. Barton
Glenn Corbett	Mack Miller
Bert Begley	Shilling
John Hedloe	Ullman
James Anderson	Strong Arm Man
Al Hill	Policeman
Kenner G. Kemp	Roller Derby Spectator
Frank Mills	Roller Derby Spectator

Gentlemen Prefer Blondes 1953 N/R, 91 min.

Genre: Musical / Comedy / Drama / Romance

Director: Howard Hawks

Cast: Jane Russell, Marilyn Monroe, Tommy Noonan, Charles Coburn, Elliott Reid, George Winslow, Marcel Dalio, Taylor Holmes, Harry Carey Jr., Norma Varden, Howard Wendell, Steven Geray, Peter Camlin, William Cabanne, Jean De Briac

Marilyn Monroe's and Jane Russell's rendition of "Diamonds are a Girl's Best Friend" highlight this musical comedy about Lorelei Lee's (Monroe) trip to Paris to meet her future rich husband, Gus Esmond (Tommy Noonan). Lorelei's best friend, Dorothy Shaw (Russell), joins her on the cruise, and they meet private detective Malone (Elliott Reid) who has been hired by Esmond's father (Taylor Holmes) to check on the honest intentions of Lorelei. They also become involved with Sir Francis Beekman (Charles Coburn) and Henry Spofford III (George Winslow) along the way and become involved in a number of mishaps.

Cast

Jane Russell	Dorothy Shaw
Marilyn Monroe	Lorelei Lee
Tommy Noonan	Gus Esmond
Charles Coburn	Sir Francis "Piggy" Beekman
Elliott Reid	Ernie Malone
George Winslow	Henry Spofford III
Marcel Dalio	Magistrate
Taylor Holmes	Mr. Esmond Sr.
Harry Carey Jr.	Winslow
Norma Varden	Lady Beekman
Howard Wendell	Watson
Steven Geray	Hotel Manager

222 MARILYN MONROE: THE QUEST FOR AN OSCAR

Peter Camlin   Gendarme
William Cabanne   Sims
Jean De Briac   Gendarme

Green Grass of Wyoming 1948 N/R, 89 min.
Genre: Family / Drama / Western
Director: Louis King
Cast: Peggy Cummins, Charles Coburn, Robert Arthur, Lloyd Nolan, Burl
Ives, Robert Adler, Will Wright, Geraldine Wall, Charles Tannen, Richard
Garrick, Marcella Becker, Herbert Heywood, Marilyn Monroe, Charles Hart

In this sequel to "My Friend Flicka" and "Thunderhead-Son of Flicka," the
story continues, but this time around the plot concentrates on the rival horse-
breeding families: the Greenways–Beaver (Charles Coburn) and his niece

Carey (Peggy Cummins)–and the Mclaughlins–Ken (Robert Arthur) and his parents Rob and Nell (Lloyd Nolan, and Geraldine Wall). Peggy and Ken fall in love, and Thunderhead and one of the Mclaughlin's mares also have a romantic exploit. Following a big race, the mare gives birth to Thunderhead's offspring, and all ends happily.

Cast

Peggy Cummins	Carey Greenway
Charles Coburn	Beaver Greenway
Robert Arthur	Ken McLaughlin
Lloyd Nolan	Rob McLaughlin
Burl Ives	Gus
Robert Adler	Joe
Will Wright	Jake Willis
Geraldine Wall	Nell McLaughlin
Charles Tannen	Dr. Kimgrough
Richard Garrick	Charlie
Marcella Becker	Fairground Rider
Herbert Heywood	Mort Johnson
Marilyn Monroe	Square Dancer
Charles Hart	Old-Timer

Home Town Story 1951 N/R, 68 min.
Genre: Drama
Director: Arthur Pierson
Cast: Jeffrey Lynn, Donald Crisp, Marjorie Reynolds, Alan Hale Jr., Marilyn Monroe, Barbara Brown, Melinda Plowman, Glenn Tryon, Byron Foulger, Griff Barnett

After losing an election, defeated politician Blake Washburn (Jeffrey Lynn) is sure that his liberal stance offended businessmen, and he was ousted because of his anti-capitalist stand. To solve his problem, Washburn takes over his uncle's newspaper in order to deal with his opponents.

How to Marry a Millionaire 1953 N/R, 95 min.
Genre: Comedy
Director: Jean Negulesco
Cast: Betty Grable, Marilyn Monroe, Lauren Bacall, David Wayne, Rory Calhoun, William Powell, Cameron Mitchell, Alexander D'Arcy, Fred Clark

Loco (Betty Grable), Pola (Marilyn Monroe), and Schatze Page (Lauren Bacall) join forces as they set out to find a marriageable millionaire.

Ladies of the Chorus 1949 N/R, 61 min.
Genre: Musical
Director: Phil Karlson
Cast: Adele Jergens, Marilyn Monroe, Rand Brooks, Nana Bryant, Eddie Garr, Steven Geray, Bill Edwards, Myron Healey, Robert Clarke, Gladys Blake

A chorus girl (Adele Jergens) is determined to prevent her daughter (Marilyn Monroe) from making the same mistakes in romance that she, herself, did years ago.

Let's Make It Legal 1951 N/R, 77 min.
Genre: Comedy
Director: Richard Sale
Cast: Claudette Colbert, Macdonald Carey, Zachary Scott, Barbara Bates, Robert Wagner, Marilyn Monroe, Frank Cady, Jim Hayward, Kathleen Freeman, Roger Moore

After an amicable divorce following 20 years of marriage, Miriam (Claudette Colbert) and Hugh (Macdonald Carey) prepare to go their separate ways–until Mariam's old love, Victor (Zachary Scott), appears on the scene and stirs up old feelings for everyone involved.

Let's Make Love 1960 N/R, 118 min.
Genre: Musical
Director: George Cukor
Cast: Marilyn Monroe, Yves Montand, Tony Randall, Frankie Vaughan, David Burns, Bing Crosby, Gene Kelly, Milton Berle, Wilfrid Hyde-White, Madge Kennedy

Marilyn Monroe singing "My Heart Belongs to Daddy" makes this light, musical comedy worthwhile. Will rich Montand get her?

Love Happy 1949 N/R, 91 min.
Genre: Comedy
Director: David Miller
Cast: Groucho Marx, Harpo Marx, Chico Marx, Ilona Massey, Vera-Ellen, Raymond Burr, Marilyn Monroe, Eric Blore, Melville Cooper, Marion Hutton

This is the last in the series of Marx Brothers' movies. Marilyn Monroe has a very small part in the film.

Love Nest 1951 N/R, 84 min.
Genre: Comedy
Director: Joseph M. Newman
Cast: June Haver, William Lundigan, Frank Fay, Marilyn Monroe, Jack Paar, Leatrice Joy

When Jim Scott (William Lundigan) returns from the Army, he finds that his wife has bought a New York apartment building, and they are the hapless landlords.

Marilyn Monroe: Beyond the Legend 1987 N/R, 60 min.
Genre: Documentary
Director: Gene Feldman, Suzette Winter
Cast: Marilyn Monroe, Richard Widmark, Robert Mitchum, Shelley Winters, Celeste Holm, Joshua Logan, Sheree North, Susan Strasberg, Don Murray

This documentary depicts the human side of ill-fated movie star Marilyn Monroe who killed herself in the early 1960s. Richard Widmark narrates.

The Misfits 1961 N/R, 124 min.

Genre: Drama

Director: John Huston

Cast: Clark Gable, Marilyn Monroe, Montgomery Clift, Thelma Ritter, Eli Wallach, Kevin McCarthy, James Barton, Estelle Winwood, Denis Shaw, Marietta Tree

A new divorcee, Roslyn Tabor (Marilyn Monroe), befriends some cowboys and falls in love with one of them–Gay Langland (Clark Gable)–in this story written by Monroe's husband, Arthur Miller. Gable's and Monroe's last film.

Monkey Business 1952 N/R, 97 min.

Genre: Comedy

Director: Howard Hawks

Cast: Cary Grant, Ginger Rogers, Charles Coburn, Marilyn Monroe, Hugh Marlowe, Henri Letondal, Robert Cornthwaite, Larry Keating, Harry Carey Jr., Douglas Spencer

Barnaby Fulton (Cary Grant) is a chemist-genius who has been working on a formula to prevent aging. A monkey accidentally mixes the correct proportions into the elixir, which ends up in the Fulton's drinking water. After Barnaby and his wife, Edwina (Ginger Rogers), start drinking the tainted water, they revert to childhood.

Niagara 1953 N/R, 89 min.

Genre: Drama

Director: Henry Hathaway

Cast: Marilyn Monroe, Joseph Cotten, Jean Peters, Max Showalter, Denis O'Dea, Don Wilson, Lurene Tuttle, Lester Matthews, Will Wright, Russell Collins

Illustrierter
Film-Kurier
CARY GRANT
GINGER ROGERS
MARILYN MONROE
Ich heisse RUDOLF
Liebling
ICH WERDE
JÜNGER
MONKEY BUSINESS
CHARLES COBURN
20th CENTURY-FOX
Regie:
HOWARD HAWKS

Rose Loomis (Marilyn Monroe) has well-laid plans to kill her husband George (Joseph Cotten), BUT as with many plans, this one goes astray-very much astray.

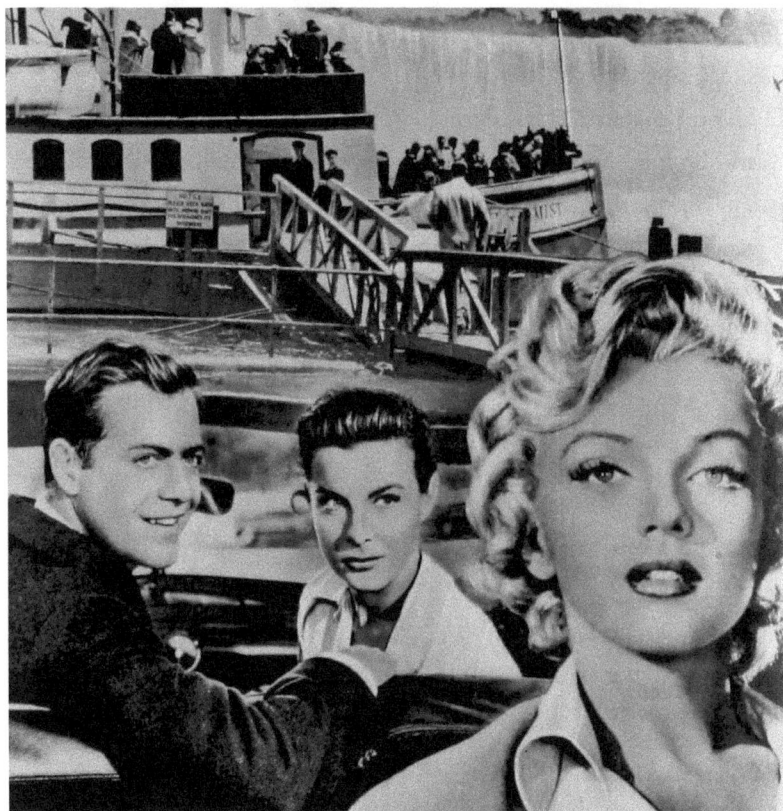

O. Henry's Full House 1952 N/R, 116 min.
Genre: Drama
Director: Henry Hathaway, Howard Hawks, Henry King, Henry Koster, Jean Negulesco
Cast: Charles Laughton, Marilyn Monroe, David Wayne, Dale Robertson, Richard Widmark, Anne Baxter, Jean Peters, Fred Allen, Oscar Levant, Jeanne Crain

John Steinbeck narrated this film consisting of five of O. Henry's classic short stories: "The Clarion Call," "The Ransom of Red Chief," "The Gift of the Magi," "The Cop and the Anthem," and "The Last Leaf."

The Prince and the Showgirl 1957 N/R, 117 min.
Genre: Comedy
Director: Laurence Olivier
Cast: Marilyn Monroe, Laurence Olivier, Sybil Thorndike, Richard Wattis, Jeremy Spenser, Esmond Knight, Maxine Audley, Paul Hardwick, Rosamund Greenwood, Andreas Malandrinos

While in London for the 1912 coronation of George V, a Balkan prince (Laurence Olivier) falls for an American showgirl (Marilyn Monroe) who aids his reconciliation with his son.

Right Cross 1950 N/R, 89 min.
Genre: Drama
Director: John Sturges
Cast: June Allyson, Dick Powell, Ricardo Montalban, Lionel Barrymore, Tom Powers, Kenneth Tobey, Teresa Celli, Barry Kelley, Mimi Aguglia, Marilyn Monroe

Verlag „Das Neue Filmprogramm" GmbH
Mannheim, Weinheimer Straße 58-60
Druck: KLEMMER-TIEFDRUCK Mannheim
Telefon 76527 · Fernschreiber 046/2156

Am nächsten Morgen sieht der Prinzregent die Welt im rosigsten Licht. Für jetzt heißt es zwar Abschiednehmen, aber in achtzehn Monaten, wenn er nicht mehr Prinzregent sein wird — wer weiß? . . . . „Auf Wiedersehen!" haucht Miss Marina, als sie — zum wievielten Male schon? zum Abschied den Hausorden angesteckt bekommt.

„NEUES FILMPROGRAMM" Die Kinozeitschrift für das Publikum
Vormals „Illustrierter Film-Kurier" und „Programm von Heute"

Dezember-Folge 1957

Eigentümer: Leminger, Spalding und Weiss. Für den Inhalt verantwortlich: R. Leminger, Wien VII, Lindengasse 43, Tel. 44 66 53. Alleinherstellungsrecht für Österreich. Nachdruck (auch auszugsweise) nur mit Erlaubnis gestattet. Rotationstiefdruck: Elbemühl AG., Wien III, Rudengasse 11.

Gesehen am: gut gefallen   mittel   schwach

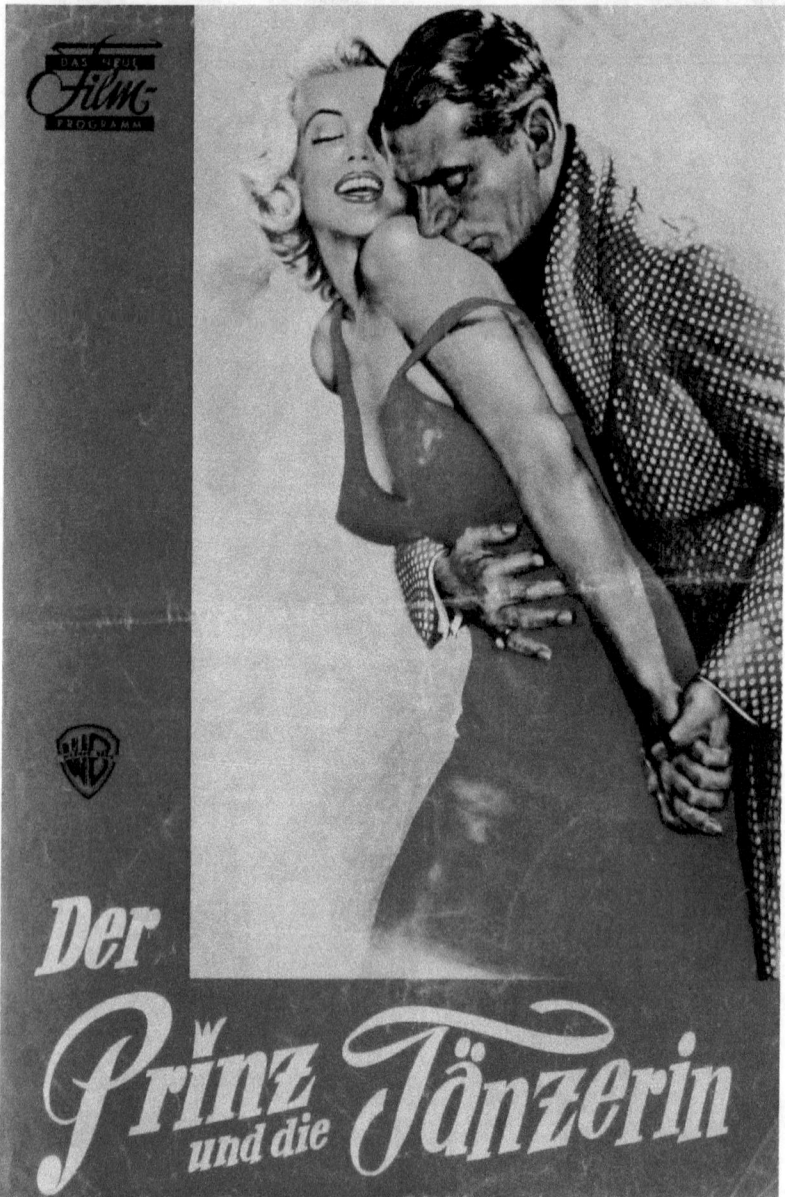

A Mexican prizefighter (Ricardo Montalban) and a sports writer (Dick Powell) vie for the attentions of the fighter's female manager (June Allyson).

River of No Return 1954 N/R, 90 min.
Genre: Western
Director: Otto Preminger
Cast: Robert Mitchum, Marilyn Monroe, Rory Calhoun, Tommy Rettig, Will Wright, Murvyn Vye, Douglas Spencer, Arthur Shields, Don Beddoe, Edmund Cobb

After being double-crossed, Matt Calder (Robert Mitchum) is left as the sole protector of his son Mark (Tommy Rettig) and Kay (Marilyn Monroe) who need help riding the rapids of a Canadian river and avoiding an Indian uprising.

Scudda Hoo! Scudda Hay! 1948 N/R, 95 min.
Genre: Comedy / Drama / Romance
Director: F. Hugh Herbert
Cast: June Haver, Lon McCallister, Walter Brennan, Anne Revere, Natalie Wood, Robert Karnes, Marilyn Monroe, Tom Tully, Ken Christy, Edward Gargan, Henry Hull, Robert Adler, Lee MacGregor, Tom Moore, Geraldine Wall

This comedy involves a young farmer, Snug Dominy (Lon McCallister) whose interest in keeping his team of mules seems to obscure all else in his life. Snug lives with his stepmother Judith (Anne Revere) who devotes herself to Snug's stepbrother Stretch (Robert Karnes). Matters rise to the fore when Snug falls in love with Rad (June Haver) who is the daughter of "Roarer" McGill (Tom Tully) who sold Snug the mules and now wants them back. Marilyn Monroe's film debut is brief–can you find her paddling a canoe?

Cast

June Haver	Rad McGill
Lon McCallister	Daniel "Snug" Dominy
Walter Brennan	Tony Maule
Anne Revere	Judith Dominy
Natalie Wood	Eufraznee "Bean" McGill
Robert Karnes	Stretch Dominy
Marilyn Monroe	Girl in Canoe
Tom Tully	Robert "Roarer" McGill
Ken Christy	Sheriff Tod Bursom
Edward Gargan	Ted
Henry Hull	Milt Dominy
Robert Adler	Mac
Lee MacGregor	Ches Forrester
Tom Moore	Judge Stillwell
Geraldine Wall	Mrs. Lucy McGill

The Seven Year Itch 1955 N/R, 105 min.

Genre: Comedy / Romance

Director: Billy Wilder

Cast: Marilyn Monroe, Tom Ewell, Evelyn Keyes, Butch Bernard, Sonny Tufts, Robert Strauss, Oskar Homolka, Marguerite Chapman, Victor Moore, Donald MacBride, Carolyn Jones, Dolores Rosedale, Dorothy Ford, Doro Merande, Ron Nyman

After seven years of marriage, Richard Sherman (Tom Ewell) and his wife (Evelyn Keyes) say a short goodbye as she leaves to spend the summer in the coolness of Maine, and he resolves to spend a boring summer in the city. Boredom is thrown to the wind when Richard meets a neighbor (Marilyn Monroe). Tom Ewell: "What happened at the office? Well, I shot Mr. Brady in the head, made violent love to Miss Morris, and set fire to 300,000 copies of 'Little Women'."

Cast

Marilyn Monroe	The Girl
Tom Ewell	Richard Sherman
Evelyn Keyes	Helen Sherman
Butch Bernard	Ricky Sherman
Sonny Tufts	Tom MacKenzie
Robert Strauss	Mr. Kruhulik
Oskar Homolka	Dr. Brubaker
Marguerite Chapman	Miss Morris
Victor Moore	Plumber
Donald MacBride	Mr. Brady
Carolyn Jones	Miss Finch

Dolores Rosedale	Elaine
Dorothy Ford	Indian Girl
Doro Merande	Waitress
Ron Nyman	Indian

Some Like It Hot 1959 N/R, 120 min.

Genre: Comedy / Romance / Musical

Director: Billy Wilder

Cast: Marilyn Monroe, Tony Curtis, Jack Lemmon, George Raft, Joe E. Brown, Joan Shawlee, Pat O'Brien, Nehemiah Persoff, George E. Stone,

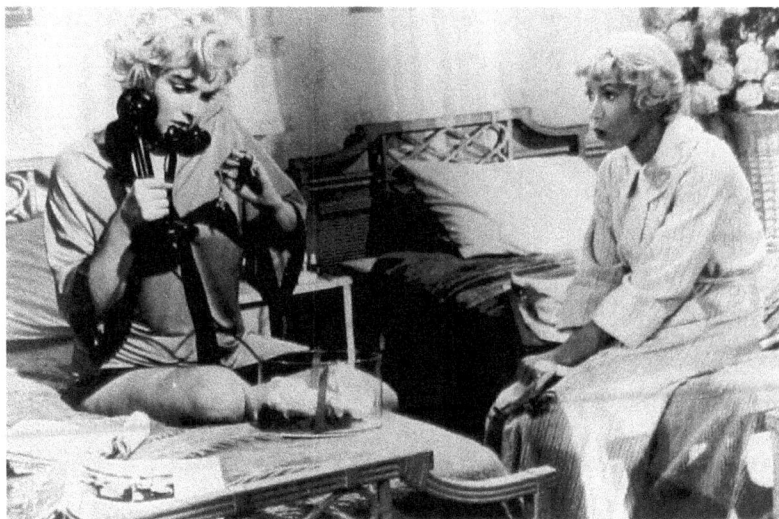

Billy Gray, Dave(1) Barry, Mike Mazurki, Harry Wilson, Beverly Wills, Tom Kennedy

Two out-of-work musicians, Joe and Jerry (Tony Curtis and Jack Lemmon) witness the St. Valentine's Day Massacre and must escape from Chicago. Their vehicle is an all-girl band, which they join disguised as women Josephine and Daphne. The fun begins as they hop on a train with their fellow band members and must keep up the disguise. Marilyn Monroe: "I always get the fuzzy end of the lollipop." The film won an Oscar for Best Costume Design and was nominated for five others, including Best Actor (Lemmon) and Director.

Cast

Marilyn Monroe	Sugar Kane
Tony Curtis	Joe/Josephine
Jack Lemmon	Jerry/Daphne
George Raft	Spats Columbo
Joe E. Brown	Osgood E. Fielding III
Joan Shawlee	Sweet Sue
Pat O'Brien	Mulligan
Nehemiah Persoff	Little Bonaparte
George E. Stone	Toothpick Charlie
Billy Gray	Sig Poliakoff
Dave(1) Barry	Beinstock
Mike Mazurki	Spats' Henchman
Harry Wilson	Spats' Henchman
Beverly Wills	Dolores
Tom Kennedy	Bouncer

There's No Business Like Show Business 1954 N/R, 117 min.

Genre: Musical

Director: Walter Lang

Cast: Ethel Merman, Marilyn Monroe, Donald O'Connor, Dan Dailey, Johnnie Ray, Mitzi Gaynor, Hugh O'Brian, Frank McHugh, Rhys Williams, Lyle Talbot

Filled with Irving Berlin songs, this is a delightful musical about a vaudeville family and their roles in show business.

A Ticket to Tomahawk 1950 N/R, 90 min.

Genre: Western

Director: Richard Sale

Cast: Dan Dailey, Anne Baxter, Rory Calhoun, Walter Brennan, Arthur Hunnicutt, Will Wright, Charles Kemper, Jack Elam, Connie Gilchrist, Marilyn Monroe

In this Comedy/Western, Johnny (Dan Dailey) is a traveling salesman who has the bad luck to be the only passenger on a train derailed by competing stagecoach personnel. Look for Marilyn Monroe as one of the chorus girls backing up Dailey's song.

We're Not Married 1952 N/R, 85 min.

Genre: Comedy

Director: Edmund Goulding

Cast: Ginger Rogers, Victor Moore, Fred Allen, Marilyn Monroe, David Wayne, Eve Arden, Paul Douglas, Eddie Bracken, Mitzi Gaynor, Louis Calhern

A number of couples are happily married–until they learn that their marriage ceremonies were not legal.

Something's Got To Give 1962

Genre: Comedy

Director: George Cukor

Cast: Dean Martin, Cyd Charisse, Tom Tryon, Phil Silvers, Steve Allen, Alexandria Heilweil,

Robert Christopher Morley, John McGiver, Grady Sutton, Eloise Hardt, Wally Cox, Marilyn Monroe

This unfinished movie would prove to be the very last time Marilyn Monroe went before the camera. In a series of ironic twists, one of them had to do with Marilyn's birthday. On June 1, 1962, Marilyn's 36th birthday she filmed a scene with Wally Cox, it was the very last time Marilyn acted in Hollywood. There are over nine hours of unseen footage in the 20th Century Fox vaults. The footage was digitally restored and 37 minutes of the film were contained in a two hour documentary. The documentary was called *Marilyn: The Final Days*, it aired on American Movie Classics, June 1, 2001, which ironically would have been Marilyn's 75th birthday. It was the very last wink, that all too famous wink that Marilyn shared with all of us, which is the most memorable part of the restored footage.

Marilyn Monroe Commemorative Stamp

First Day Of Issue Ceremony
Universal Studios Hollywood • Universal City, California
June 1, 1995

Master of Ceremonies
Army Archerd

Welcome	Universal Studios Hollywood
Remarks	Anna Strasberg
	Estate of Marilyn Monroe
Dedication of Stamp	Marvin Runyon
	Postmaster General, CEO
	United States Postal Service

— Honored Guests —

Honorable Tirso del Junco
Vice Chairman, Board of Governors
United States Postal Service

Michael Deas
Artist of the Marilyn Monroe Stamp

Richard Ordoñez
District Manager
Customer Service and Sales
United States Postal Service

Citizens' Stamp Advisory Committee
Michael Brock
Karl Malden
Stephen T. McLin
Virginia Noelke
John Sawyer III

Dale Herbert
Postmaster
North Hollywood, California

CHAPTER 10

Unique Facts

"I'm not interested in money, I just want to be wonderful."

THERE ARE SO MANY INTERESTING FACTS about Marilyn Monroe that it would take a two volume set of books to list only half of them. Here are some you might not be aware of but will add to your enjoyment of being a fan of Marilyn.

Marilyn was by no means a dumb blonde, her IQ was an amazing 168!

Marilyn took literature classes at UCLA.

Marilyn was an author, she even wrote her autobiography, *My Story*, however the book was not published until ten years after her death.

Original artwork for the first U.S. Marilyn postage stamp.

Marilyn's 1954 ID card she used to entertain the troops was sold at auction for $57,000.

Marilyn loved dogs, her favorite named Maf, was a Maltese terrier given to her by none other than Frank Sinatra. Two Polaroids of the terrier sold at a Christie's auction for $344,000, back in 1999.

Marilyn's first dog she owned as a little girl was named Tippy, it was also the name of the dog she owned when she died.

Marilyn's gown she wore when she sang Happy Birthday to President Kennedy sold for $128,000, at the same Christie's auction in 1999.

Marilyn's white dress in The Seven Year Itch sold for $5.5 million in 2011.

Forever Marilyn is a 26 foot tall statue made of 34,000 pounds of stainless steel and aluminum of the scene depicted in The Seven Year Itch. The statue was originally on display in Chicago but is now in Palm Springs, California.

Marilyn's white grand baby piano was purchased by Mariah Carey for $662,500.

Marilyn was paid $50 to model for the famous photo which was published in Issue #1 of Playboy Magazine. She was named the Sweetheart of the Month back then, before the centerfolds were known as Playmates of the month.. Hugh Hefner purchased the photo for $500.

Marilyn's burial vault is located at Westwood Memorial Park in Los Angeles. Hugh Hefner purchased the vault next to Marilyn's in 1992 for $78,000. The vault above Marilyn's has received bids in excess of 4.4 million dollars.

Marilyn's crypt had roses sent three times a week for 20 years by Joe DiMaggio. A well known fact....but what you might not know is that it was a request made by Marilyn before she died.

MARILYN MONROE

Marilyn did not own any expensive jewelry, even though she is always associated with the tune she made famous, Diamonds are a Girl's Best Friend.

Marilyn included Albert Einstein on her list of attractive men. She admired intelligent men.

Marilyn met Nikita Khrushchev, Russia's then president and the two discussed the famous novel, *The Brothers Karamazov*.

There are more collectables with the image and likeness of Marilyn than any other celebrity including, famous Americans as well as sports figures.

Each and every year since she died, Marilyn is on the top ten list of revenue generated by deceased celebrities.

In 1995 Marilyn was featured on a 32 cent United States postage stamp. More recently when the United States Treasury ran a contest to redesign paper currency, Marilyn's image was a selection on the fifty dollar bill.

MARILYN

CHAPTER 11

Eulogy

"We should all start to live before we get too old. Fear is stupid.
So are regrets."

WHEN THE FINAL ANALYSIS IS DONE after so many different evaluations of
the overall talent of Marilyn Monroe it is a certainty that everyone will agree
she was more than just a sexy dumb blond. Her talent was overlooked and in
the last four movies that she starred in there can be no doubt that her performances deserved recognition in the form of an Oscar nomination. Maybe
there was perhaps only one performance that should have been nominated,
or maybe two or more should have been considered. The sad reality is that
now that those performances are over and cannot be considered for an Oscar,
the body of work should be at least re-evaluated and considered. Each one of

those performances were unique and had many great glimpses of what it takes to get noticed and never forgotten.

Eulogy

In her own lifetime she created a myth of what a poor girl from a deprived background could attain. For the entire world she became a symbol of the eternal feminine. But I have no words to describe the myth and the legend. I did not know this Marilyn Monroe.

We, gathered here today, knew only Marilyn - a warm human being, impulsive and shy, sensitive and in fear of rejection, yet ever avid for life and reaching out for fulfillment. I will not insult the privacy of your memory of her - a privacy she sought and treasured - by trying to describe her whom you knew to you who knew her. In our memories of her she remains alive, not only a shadow on a screen or a glamorous personality.

For us Marilyn was a devoted and loyal friend, a colleague constantly reaching for perfection. We shared her pain and difficulties and some of her joys. She was a member of our family. It is difficult to accept that her zest for life has been ended by this dreadful accident.

Despite the height and brilliance she had attained on the screen, she was planning for the future: she was looking forward to participating in the many exciting things she had planned. In her eyes and in mine her career was just beginning. The dream of her talent, which she nurtured as a child, was not a mirage. When she first came to me I was amazed at the startling sensitivity which she possessed and which had remained fresh and undimmed, struggling to express itself despite the life to which she had been subjected. Others were as physically beautiful as she was, but there was obviously something more in her, something people saw and recognized in her performances and with which they identified. She had a luminous quality - a combination of wistfulness, radiance, yearning - to set her apart and yet make everyone wish to be part of it, to share in the childish naivete which was at once so shy and yet so vibrant.

This quality was even more evident when she was on stage. I am truly sorry that the public who loved her did not have the opportunity to see her as we did, in many the roles that foreshadowed what she would have become. Without a doubt she would have been one of the great actresses of the stage.

Now it is all at an end. I hope that her death will stir sympathy and understanding for a sensitive artist and woman who brought joy and pleasure to the world.

I cannot say goodbye, Marilyn never liked goodbyes, but in a peculiar way she had of turning things around so that they faced reality - I will say au revoir. For the country she has gone, we must all someday visit.

—*Marilyn's funeral eulogy by Lee Strasberg (August 9, 1962)*

La 20th CENTURY

CHAPTER 12

Epilogue

"After you see her smile, watch her walk, hear her sigh and whisper, gaze into those eyes, can you ever forget her? I know the answer. You as I never will."
—James Turiello

THERE EXISTS ONLY A FEW ACCOUNTS of the serious side of Marilyn Monroe regarding her acting skills during her early days in Hollywood. It was during this period at the very onset of her short career that she became extremely diligent while practicing the art of being a serious actress. It all began when Marilyn spotted Joseph Schenck, the founder of 20th Century Fox Studios. Marilyn simply smiled at him, and Mr. Schenck immediately struck up a conversation. It can be said that if Marilyn would have smiled at any man, the results would always be the same. He was actually being driven in his limousine and he told his chauffeur to stop immediately. During this brief encounter the young Marilyn developed a very unique relationship with this Hollywood icon. Even though Mr. Schenck was no longer the head of 20th

Century Fox, he still was an executive producer. He was forced to relinquish his position due to a jail sentence he served as a result of various labor unrest and payoffs. Before he Darryl Zanuck to create 20th Century Pictures, he and his brothers owned Palisades Amusement Park, in Englewood Cliffs, New Jersey. This was an iconic East Coast attraction that was visited on a regular basis by the author. A unique characteristic of this amusement park was the salt water swimming pool, one of the largest of its era, complete with a waterfall, waves and even a sandy beach. It was on one of the author's visits that none other than Buster Crabbe who frequented the pool, actually taught the author how to swim. The park closed in the early 1970's, and the Schenck Brothers concentrated on the business of making movies. Getting back to Marilyn's encounter with Joseph Schenck, he was so impressed with not only her looks but her unique personality that he invited her to a dinner party at his mansion. Marilyn was a relative unknown among the vast circle of Mr. Schenck's friends but she quickly became a regular at these frequent dinner parties. It was during this period of Marilyn Monroe's Hollywood era that she became a very good and close friend of Joseph Schenck. This friendship was most likely fostered by the high intellect that Marilyn had. Of course the rumors of their relationship was discussed in most of the gossip columns but the rumors were just rumors. Marilyn would spend hours and hours with Joseph and they discussed his life and her ambition to be a great actress. Mr. Schenck was almost 70 years old when he met Marilyn, and she was just 21 years old. It was also reported that it was Mr. Schenck who actually obtained Marilyn's 1948 Columbia Pictures contract from Harry Cohn, the head of Columbia. This led to Marilyn's first co-starring role in Ladies of the Chorus. Even though Marilyn later went back under contract with Fox, Joseph Schenck always made sure his very close friend was treated properly. Many years later Marilyn never forgot how this great man, Joseph Schenck always treated her with the utmost respect and dignity. She visited him often as he became ill and bed ridden, only months before he died in 1961. On one such occasion while she was returning home with her publicist, Rupert Allan said Marilyn cried openly, her respect for him went far beyond what he could have done for her career. Way back in 1947 Fox actually dropped Marilyn's option with the studio. They did not completely sever their ties with Marilyn, her photos were always used extensively at various publicity functions. These functions were very common in Hollywood during the 1940's. Unfortunately for Marilyn Fox had another blonde actress in their stable. She was extremely popular and it was due partly because of the popularity of her pin-up photos. Her name was Betty Grable but unlike Marilyn who at the time was limited to publicity photos and an occasional small role, Betty Grable was a seasoned movie star and the most famous pinup of World War II. It was Marilyn's limited show business background which was the main reason why the studio choose to pass on Marilyn as a successor to Betty Grable. They soon became friends and Betty Grable was always protective of Marilyn and showed no resentment even though she knew Marilyn was the new blonde and most likely her successor. During this early period of her career in Hollywood, Marilyn decided to try her skill at performing on the stage. It was almost the same time in his career that Errol Flynn also decided to try his hand at stage productions and it eventually led to Errol making his way from the English stage to Hollywood. Marilyn found out about The Bliss Hayden Miniature Theater in Beverly Hills from ads they ran for casting calls. When Marilyn answered one of the ads, she was given the second lead in a lighthearted spoof of Hollywood, entitled Glamour Preferred. The play only ran for three weeks but it was still another venue that created attention, for the ambitious and very determined, Marilyn. The Bliss Hayden Theater was responsible for helping launch the careers of many other Hollywood hopefuls. Some of the most famous names to have passed through their doors were, Doris Day, Debbie Reynolds, Veronica Lake, Jon Hall, Craig Stevens and Mamie Van Doren. This would prove to be the only time in Marilyn's career that she acted on the small stage. One of the owners of the theater, Lela Bliss remarked many years later when asked about Marilyn, "that she could have played anything."

Marilyn even took classes at a professional acting lesson company, The Actors Lab. This ambitious endeavor lasted a full two years while Marilyn was actually quite busy switching between two studios. It can be noted she paid for the lessons with the little money she had.

There are many great actors and actresses who just like Marilyn have been overlooked by the Academy, one will never fully understand or uncover the reasons behind their decisions, to ignore their achievements, but it is certain that the time to recognize Marilyn and her fellow colleagues is way overdue.

Acknowledgments

Photo & Poster Credits:

Art Harvey, Vintage Posters & Stills - New Jersey

Cinema Collectables - Henderson, Nevada

El Tropico, Movie Star Stills - Isla Verde, P.R.

Cinema Images - Los Angeles

Private Designs - New York

Also:

Doug Turiello - he suggested the title of the series The Quest for an Oscar

Martin Grams - author and host of The Mid-Atlantic Nostalgia Convention

James Rosin - author and actor

Jack Marino - host of L.A. Talk Radio, movie producer and director of
  Forgotten Heroes

Mike Creager - host of Amazicon Convention, and dear friend

Carol Duke – she suggested Marilyn instead of Tony Curtis

  Dedicated to Chris Turiello, my son who makes movies and will one day
be a revered cinematographer. Doug Turiello, my son who cooks up a storm
and who is destined to be a famous chef. Jimmy Turiello, my son who is famous in his own right and known as "The Mustang Maniac". Patrick Turiello,
my dearest son who creates unique apparel at his studio, LAYERXLAYER.
My loving daughters, Amanda, the dedicated school teacher and Dawn the
soft drink executive both of whom I am extremely proud of. My Dad and
Mom, responsible for giving me a loving and inspirational upbringing.

About the Author

Jim Turiello grew up in Washington Heights, New York where his favorite pastimes were playing football, baseball, basketball, and bowling. In his spare time he went to the many movie palaces that were common in upper New York City. He also took the 'A' train to Times Square in the city to catch the latest releases. He claims to have seen all of the following movies over 100 times and these are also his top ten list of great movies. The Godfather I & II, Jaws, The Adventures of Robin Hood, (Errol Flynn version), King Kong, (1933), The Mummy, (Boris Karloff), The Creature from the Black Lagoon, The Treasure of the Sierra Madre, The Thing, (1951), Some Like It Hot, Rebel Without A Cause, Giant, Rocky, Casino, Goodfellas, Dirty Harry...wait a minute that's way more than ten! I guess you are getting the picture, Jim loves movies as well as Flash Gordon and Tim Tyler serials. He had the distinction of being a lead soprano in the world famous St Patrick's Cathedral Choir.

Jim is an avid football fan of the San Diego Chargers and even writes a weekly sports column for BrianSmithRadio.com. From the 1960's to 2005 he was a regular on numerous sports programs in the tri-state area. As a prolific writer his contributions to music, movie and collectable magazines are too numerous to mention. Jim also produced a unique trading card set, The James Dean Collection, that included 50 photos of James Dean with an original biographical story that ran on the reverse of each card. The card set received rave reviews when it was released and is still available at the James Dean Gallery in Fairmount, Indiana, James Dean's hometown. The next book in the series will be aptly titled, *James Dean: The Quest for an Oscar*, look for it next year and sometime in the future his unpublished novel, *Badge in the Tunnel*.

Jim loves to travel and has been to almost all of the Caribbean Islands but now spends most of his time in Viva Las Vegas. He has two daughters and four sons and lives with his soul mate, Ebie who coincidentally shares a birthday with Errol Flynn.

Marilyn's first dog was named 'Tippy,' the name of her last dog was also named 'Tippy,' when Jim was ten years old his Dad gave him a puppy, Jim named him 'Tippy,' they say you can't make this stuff up.

The author in 1962, really!

The story behind the picture: When Jim was at one of the many conventions where he is a guest promoting his books the following occurred. Another guest at the convention had a unique photo machine that was able to literally put "you" in any existing photo. The gentleman who owned the machine was named Morton and when he saw Jim's High School graduation photo Morton remarked, " you look just like Elvis." Jim replied, "I know, that was my nickname in High School, College and wherever I worked." Morton knew Jim was writing a book about Marilyn Monroe and he had a foreign picture of Elvis and Marilyn so he took Jim's graduation photo and substituted Jim in Elvis's place.

A faded still from Marilyn›s last movie, as you know it was never completed.

......how could they overlook Marilyn, Marilyn who had only one true love, the camera, the camera who remained faithful to Marilyn right up to the end, and Marilyn never ever disappointed her one true love, Marilyn sparkled one last time......and a long time before that last time Marilyn sparkled in one impeccable moment unrehearsed in The Asphalt Jungle. Marilyn came of age with this one dramatic moment, "Haven't you bothered me enough you big banana head? Just try breaking my door." However no matter how many times you watch that scene, the camera and Marilyn were as one, an unimpeachable performance......

"In the external scheme of things, shining moments are as brief as the twinkling of an eye, yet such twinklings are what eternity is made of--moments when we human beings can say "I love you," "I'm proud of you," "I forgive you," " I'm grateful for you." That's what eternity is made of: invisible imperishable good stuff." —*Fred Rogers*

......"Marilyn and her performances were "good stuff"......"great stuff".
—*James Turiello*

Index

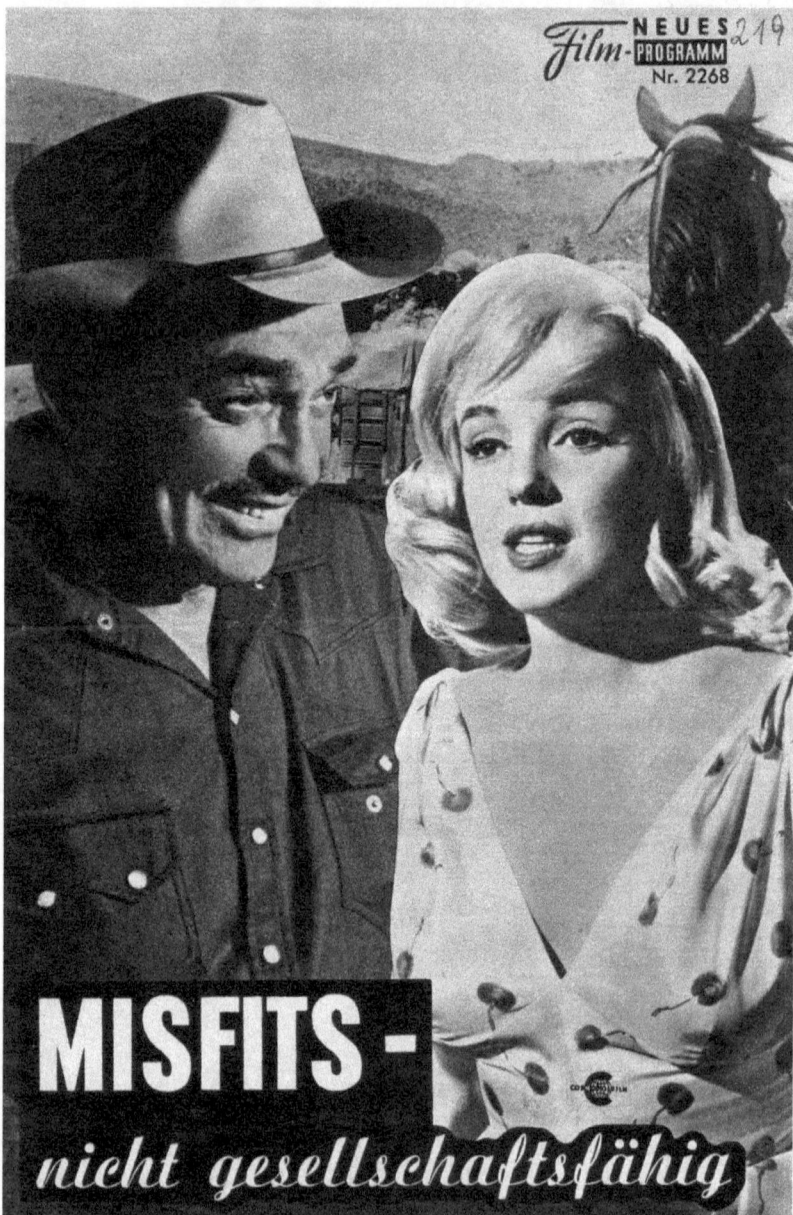

Loew, Marcus, 124
Loews' 175th Street, 86
Loews' Jersey Theater, 88
Loews' Kings Theater, 88
Loews' Paradise Theater, 88
Loews' Valencia, Theater, 88
Logan, Joshua, 18, 155, 157, 213, 227
Loren, Frederick, 132
Loren, Sophia, 137, 170
Lorre, Peter, 129
Love Affair, 139
Love Field, 139
Love Happy, 15, 35, 36, 227
Love Nest, 39, 60, 227
Love with the Proper Stranger, 133
Lumet, Sidney, 6
Lupino, Ida, 130
Lust For Life, 137

M
MacMurray, Fred, 130
Madison Square Garden, 102
Maf, 258
Maggie Paul, 133
Maine, 143, 242
Maltese, 258
Manhattan, 143
Mankiewicz, Joseph L., 18, 44, 207
Marcellus, Gallio, 133
Marchand, Colette, 57
Marie Allen, 133
Marilyn Monroe Productions, 157
Marjorie Lawrence, 134
Marshall Jed Cooper, 132
Martin, Dean, xiii, 253
Marx, Groucho, vii, 15, 35, 36, 227
Mary McLeod, 133
Mason, James, 130, 136
Mason, Marsha, 131, 133
Massey, Raymond, 131
Mastroianni, Marcello, 131, 137
Maxwell, John, 40, 211, 213
Mayan, 88
Mayer, Louis B., 124
McIntire, John, 40, 211, 212

thoden die Pferdefänger vorgehen. Vergeblich bittet sie Gaylord, die mit Flugzeug und Auto gejagten und mit einem Lasso gefangenen und gefesselten Pferde zu befreien. Da erbarmt sich sich als der brutalste von allen entpuppt, nichts von einem Aufgeben der Jagd wissen will. Perce schneidet in einem unbewachten Moment die Fesseln der Pferde durch und jagt sie zurück in die Berge. Im letzten Moment kommt Gaylord dazu — es gelingt ihm nach ungeheuren Schwierigkeiten, den Leithengst der Herde noch einmal zu fangen. Doch denn als er zu seiner eigenen Rechtfertigung gezeigt hat, daß er stärker ist als die Tiere, schenkt er mit dieser Tat Gaylords die Entscheidung gefallen — wortlos setzt sie sich neben ihn ans Steuer seines Wagens — und als er losfährt, legt sie vertrauensvoll ihren Kopf an seine Schulter.

März-Folge   „NEUES FILMPROGRAMM"   1961

Eigentümer: Leminger, Spalding und Weiss. Für den Inhalt verantwortlich: R. Leminger, Wien VII, Lindengasse 43 Tel. 44 66 53. Alleinherstellungsrecht für Österreich. Nachdruck (auch auszugsweise) nur mit Erlaubnis gestattet. Abonnement: 40 Nummern zu S 18.— (ca. 12mal jährlich) Rotationstiefdruck. Elbemühl AG., Wien XXIII, Altmannsdorfer Straße 154-156

Watch for James Turiello's next book

JAMES DEAN: THE QUEST FOR AN OSCAR

coming soon!

www.ingramcontent.com/pod-product-compliance
Lightning Source LLC
Chambersburg PA
CBHW061559110426
42742CB00038B/1671